SIGNS OF GLORY

SIGNS OF GLORY

Richard Holloway

The Seabury Press / New York

1983
The Seabury Press
815 Second Avenue
New York, N.Y. 10017

Printed in the United States of America

ISBN 0-8164-2412-8

Grateful acknowledgment is hereby made to Random House, Inc.,
for permission to reprint lines from "Musée des Beaux Arts," by
W. H. Auden. The lines are taken from *W. H. Auden: Collected
Poems,* by W. H. Auden, copyright © 1945 by W. H. Auden.

To

The Society of the Sacred Mission
in thanksgiving for the men it
trained for the priesthood at
Kelham

CONTENTS

ACKNOWLEDGEMENTS

I must thank my secretary, Martha Mitchell, for her uncomplaining labours in typing this book. I ought also to thank my colleagues, Robert Malm and Geoffrey Hahneman, for putting up with a rector who spends every Monday hunched over a typewriter. I am grateful for their support and friendship.

The book is dedicated to the Society of the Sacred Mission, with particular gratitude for the years I spent at Kelham and in general thanksgiving for the many priests in the Anglican Communion who were trained by the Society. If any of them should read this book, I hope they will pause for a moment and remember singing 'Christ the fair glory of the holy angels', on many a Michaelmas Day at Kelham; I hope they will recall sung compline during Lent, and Kelham beans after the Three Hours on Good Friday; above all, I hope they still live under the strong and grieving face of the Christ on the great rood.

The Church of the Advent   *Richard Holloway*
30 Brimmer Street   *February 1982*
Boston

Thanks are due to the following for permission to reproduce material from copyright sources:

Constable and Co: *Mediaeval Latin Lyrics* by Helen Waddell.

Faber and Faber: 'Musée des Beaux Arts' from *Collected Poems* by W. H. Auden.

The majority of Scripture quotations in this publication are from the Revised Standard Version of the Bible copyrighted 1971 and 1952 by the Division of Christian Education of the National Council of the Churches of Christ in the USA.

Chapter 1

MIRACLE

There are many ways to study Christianity. It can, for instance, be studied and defined as a group in society or as a movement in history. However, in its own essential self-understanding, Christianity is the abiding presence of Jesus Christ. And Jesus Christ is the expression, in history, of the everlasting God, whose ways are unsearchable. In Chesterton's words, in Jesus Christ, 'heaven has descended into the world of matter; the supreme spiritual power is now operating in the machinery of matter, dealing miraculously with the bodies and souls of men'. Christianity, therefore, is frankly and defiantly miraculous. In spite of the efforts of some of its adherents in every generation, it is not possible to conform Christianity to the more naturalistic patterns of other philosophies. It is too embarrassingly specific for that. Christianity claims that its origin lies in a specific and unique in-breaking of God into history. This is the universal claim of the New Testament books. For instance, the Letter to the Hebrews says: 'In many and various ways God spoke of old to our fathers by the prophets; but in these last days he has spoken to us by a Son, whom he appointed the heir of all things, through whom also he created the world. He reflects the glory of God and bears the very stamp of his nature, upholding the universe by his word of power' (Hebrews 1:1–3). The author of this book makes a quite clear distinction between Christianity and what came before. The distinction still holds. Christianity is not based on the abstractions or generalities, however wise, of any human beings. It is, in essence, a Word spoken, at last, by God himself. John makes this claim even more explicit. In the prologue to his Gospel he tells us that the Word, which was the creative principle in creation, and was itself the very reality of God, 'became flesh and dwelt among us'. Paul is just as specific. Jesus Christ, he says, 'is

1

the image of the invisible God, the first-born of all creation; for in him all things were created, in heaven and on earth, visible and invisible, whether thrones or dominions or principalities or authorities—all things were created through and for him. He is before all things, and in him all things hold together. He is the head of the body, the church; he is the beginning, the first-born from the dead, that in everything he might be pre-eminent. For in him all the fulness of God was pleased to dwell, and through him to reconcile to himself all things, whether on earth or in heaven, making peace by the blood of his cross' (Colossians 1:15–20).

Christians, however, do not halt at this logically unverifiable claim about the entrance of God into history in the person of Jesus Christ. Our hope is grounded in this event, of course, but we go on to make a further claim. We claim that the real presence of God in Christ is a present reality, as well as a reality in the past. Christianity *is* Jesus Christ. It is his abiding presence in history, however elusive we may find that presence to be. It is difficult to find an analogy for this contemporary experience of Jesus. The usual analogies all locate the experience in some act of remembering, in a calling to mind of something that is not now present. That is why they fail to illustrate the real nature of Christian experience. The only thing that really illuminates the Christian experience is the experience itself. This is why philosophy has often pronounced the death of Christianity. But from the point of view of philosophy, Christianity has never really been born. It is impossible to transpose the Christian claim, in its essence, into the coinage of philosophical discourse. The heart of the Christian experience is untranslateable into logic. Nevertheless, there is a partial analogy which may take us some way in explaining the nature of the Christian's experience of Jesus. The experience of performing a piece of music written many years ago is a partial analogy of the experience of Jesus today. Each performance makes the original composition as present now as it was when it was written, because music, of all human activities, comes closest to an expression of the timeless. This analogy helps us in two ways. First of all, in music there is a real transcending of time, which makes the genius of Mozart absolutely contemporary. Secondly, that real presence of the musician's genius is only achieved by an act of obedience to the text we have received. We may not like Mozart any longer. If so, we stop playing him. If, however, it is Mozart we are claiming to play, then we must submit to the authority of the text he left, and not substitute a new composition of our own in its place.

Christianity, then, claims that in Jesus Christ God broke decisively into history. It also claims that the presence of Jesus is still mediated to us in three ways. Three actualities have been handed down to us, which authoritatively bear the abiding presence. If we continue our musical analogy, we can think of them as three movements or modes by which the same melody is expressed. As with the music, though there may be some variation in interpretation, the primary response is one of submission or obedience to something that exists in its own right. The three modes of Christ's presence are the ecclesiastical, the sacramental and the scriptural. Christ is mediated to us through Church, Sacrament and Scripture.

And anyone knows how ambiguous these modes of revelation are. It is the easiest thing in the world to stop at what is presented to our senses, and assume that that's all there is. The Gospels tell us that this is exactly what they did with Jesus: 'Is not this the carpenter's son?' The natural explanation is always the easiest. In this case, however, it happens to miss the whole point. If faith befriends our outward sense, we recognize that the material has become the vehicle of the divine presence.

Of the three modes of revelation, the New Testament writings are by far the most powerful and versatile. To a certain extent, too, they judge and interpret the other modes. While we certainly encounter Jesus in Church and Sacrament, therefore, it is above all in the Scriptures that we can expect to meet him. And here the ambiguities still reign. Obviously, we see here words written upon a page. We know, too, something about when and where they were written. We may spend a lot of time trying to account for what is said. We may even draw a number of edifying moral conclusions from what we read.

We can do all or any of these things and still miss the point. We have not met Jesus. No real encounter has taken place. For that to happen, we have to surrender our inquisitive authority over the text and submit to its authority over us. We have to wait for it to show its meaning to us, rather than proceed immediately with our own objections to it. And this has nothing to do with technical questions of fundamentalism or inerrancy. Technical questions of that sort

3

are as irrelevant to the real issue as were disputes about the birth-place of the Messiah among the hearers of Jesus. The issue does not lie there. It lies in an encounter between Him and Us. There are many ways of avoiding that encounter, but none has proved more effective than haggling over the historical status of the Gospels. It is as though a man were to step forward and say, 'I am the Son of God', and we were to reply, 'But you're only five feet tall, and, besides, your hair is red'.

Of the New Testament writers, none is less compromising than the author of the Fourth Gospel in his description of the nature of Jesus Christ and the claim he made upon human lives. Nor is any New Testament writer more aware than he of the many ways in which human beings miss the point about Jesus, either deliberately or subconsciously. John knows that the easiest way to avoid facing the claim made by Jesus is to divert the action away from the self onto some neutral theological topic. Nicodemus took refuge in some heavy philosophical sarcasm. He avoided the challenge by diverting the discussion onto the metaphor by which the challenge was conveyed: 'How can a man be born when he is old? Can he enter a second time into his mother's womb and be born?' (John 3:4). The woman of Samaria did it, too. She deflected the challenge of Jesus from her own life, onto a brisk discussion of the religious differences between Jews and Samaritans: 'Sir, I perceive that you are a prophet. Our fathers worshipped on this mountain; and you say that in Jerusalem is the place where men ought to worship' (John 4:19–20). John shows Jesus cutting through all our diversionary chatter: 'What is that to you? Follow me!' (John 21:22).

That is still his challenge to us, and we are still as tempted as any men ever were to avoid it, by shifting the discussion onto the safe neutrality of historical or theological debate. The situation has not altered. God makes his approach to us still, in his Son, through the mediation of the Scriptures. And the ambiguity of his approach offers us many chances of escape: 'Is not this Joseph's son?' 'How can a man be born when he is old?' 'Sir, I perceive that you are a prophet. Our fathers worshipped on this mountain . . .' We create a diversion, and then tiptoe away, hoping our retreat will be un-detected. If you do that often enough, you can safely avoid the challenge of Jesus, perhaps for ever.

In what follows in this book, I want to try to make it possible to hear the challenge of Jesus. I want to listen to what he says and does. I have used the present tense deliberately. The only use for the New Testament that I am really interested in now is as a vehicle for mediating the real presence of Jesus. He draws near to us still, in these pages, if we can but find the right way to pay attention. For this purpose, I want to make use of the seven great miracles in John's Gospel. These events are of enormous significance in John's account of Jesus Christ. He calls them 'signs'. By that word he seems to mean that each event is both a miracle and a parable, or, as they used to say, each is 'a wonder with a meaning in it'.

As you would expect, people argue about the historical status of these events. Well, there really is not much you can say about that, I'm afraid. You inevitably begin with certain assumptions. If you do not accept the possibility of miracles, then there is an end to it. John is clearly offering us what he takes to be history, but it is history with a depth and significance that is far beyond the ordinary. People often cling to that with relief. They do not believe these miracles happened, but they are happy to meditate upon their inward meaning! They reject the miracle, though they are more than happy to accept the parable which the miracle conveys. Well, even that might be enough, if it gets us to pay attention. My own position is simpler. It seems quite obvious to me that Christianity is miraculous and supernatural through and through, or it is nothing. The passages from Hebrews and Colossians which I quoted earlier make this quite explicit. In contradistinction to other types of religious philosophy which are possible to human beings, Christianity has always claimed that there has been a quite specific historical intervention by God, not in terms of general laws, nor by means of vague influences, but by an irruption of the timeless into time, by taking on of flesh by the Godhead. The Christian faith is miraculous through and through, if by miracle we mean an event which breaks the patterns of nature and history as we know them. That, anyway, is what we need, or so the Bible believes. It is the human predicament which calls forth from God a series of saving interventions, though, as I have said repeatedly, these actions of God are all veiled in ambiguity.

The first premise of the Christian faith is miraculous, then. It seems to me that to accept the incarnation of the Son of God in the human flesh of Mary's son, and to reject the miracles he wrought is, as he himself would have said, 'to swallow the camel and strain out the gnat'. No, I have no difficulty with miracles. My difficulty has always been with believing in God at all.

Each of John's miracles is, like Jesus himself, ambiguous or two-dimensional. Like the sacraments, they have an outward and visible element, and an inward and spiritual meaning. The external event is the vehicle, the bearer of the meaning or message; it creates a disclosure of the veiled nature of God. People today have little difficulty in accepting the inward meaning. They are used to spiritualizing the gospel, having a peculiar and fastidious opposition to the idea that God can actually intervene in the material order. Well, as I have just pointed out, this really is the heart of the Christian claim. We do claim that God intervened decisively in the person of Jesus Christ. Moreover, this divine interaction with the material and historical is the very foundation of John's Gospel. It is from John that we have the famous statement, 'The Word became flesh and dwelt among us.' It is the Word made flesh who is the worker of these wonders, but, though John takes their miraculous character for granted, he wants us to penetrate to the meaning they embody.

But let me say one final word about these events as miracles. Each of the seven miracles involves a concentration of divine power. Each short-circuits a process which happens anyway, although it usually takes longer. We are seeing here, therefore, a kind of miniaturizing or micro-processing of a permanent divine activity. This is the point made by C. S. Lewis.

> Every year as part of the natural order, God makes wine. He does so by creating a vegetable organism that can turn water, soil and sunlight into a juice which will, under proper conditions, become wine . . . Once, and in one year only, God, now incarnate, short circuits the process: makes wine in a moment: uses earthenware jars instead of vegetable fibres to hold the water.

Each event, moreover, is, in some sense, a recapitulation of the primal mystery of the incarnation. In each of the seven miraculous events, the reality of the incarnation is applied to a specific situation, and discloses the effect of the divine power upon human need. Each of these seven events, then, is the gospel of the incarnation in miniature. We must confront them in the text as they were, as far as we are able, and then go on to something far more important:

6

we must meditate upon them with an eager and submissive expectation, until each event becomes a vehicle for the disclosure of Jesus to us.

Chapter 2

TRANSFORMATION

On the third day there was a marriage at Cana in Galilee, and
the mother of Jesus was there; Jesus also was invited to the
marriage, with his disciples. When the wine gave out, the mother
of Jesus said to him, 'They have no wine.' And Jesus said to her,
'O woman, what have you to do with me? My hour has not yet
come.' His mother said to the servants, 'Do whatever he tells
you.' Now six stone jars were standing there, for the Jewish rites
of purification, each holding twenty or thirty gallons. Jesus said
to them, 'Fill the jars with water.' And they filled them up to the
brim. He said to them, 'Now draw some out, and take it to the
steward of the feast.' So they took it. When the steward of the
feast tasted the water now become wine, and did not know where
it came from (though the servants who had drawn the water
knew), the steward of the feast called the bridegroom and said to
him, 'Every man serves the good wine first; and when men have
drunk freely, then the poor wine; but you have kept the good
wine until now.' This, the first of his signs, Jesus did at Cana in
Galilee, and manifested his glory; and his disciples believed in
him.

John 2:1–11

It was a simple country wedding which had probably been going
on for several days. Jesus, we read, was invited to the wedding.
There is just a suggestion in the text that he arrived late with his
disciples. His mother's approach to him suggests that his arrival
might have been the occasion of the embarrassing discovery that
the wine had run out. Certainly, several late arrivals at the wedding
feast could easily cause something of a crisis, especially if the feast
had been running its enthusiastic course for some time. The text
hints that the mother of Jesus has been there from the beginning,

possibly as a close relative or friend. Her approach to Jesus with the information that the wine had failed implies that she was involved in the arrangements. 'They have no wine.' Next, there follows a mysterious exchange. 'Woman, what have you to do with me? My hour has not yet come.' There is no curtness in the question. It is the form of address that Jesus will use from the cross. 'Woman, behold thy son'. It is impossible to define the precise force of the words spoken by Jesus to his mother at Cana, but there is in them an element of distancing, on his part. There is no rudeness, but there is a subtle yet firm declaration of independent authority. This is part of the paradox and ambiguity of the nature of Jesus, which must have been felt with peculiar force by his mother. It is not possible to possess Jesus and use him to consecrate or validate any of our schemes and institutions. He is always, in a real sense, someone who stands over and to some extent against us. Even in his most tender relationships with us, Jesus requires the same obedience from us that he offered to his Father. There is, therefore, more than a hint of austerity in his words to Mary. It does us no harm to feel just a faint breath of the wintry summons of God, even in the warm Maytime of this country wedding. This word to Mary should caution us against any attempt to patronize Jesus or recruit him for our own interests.

Whatever Mary felt in her heart, she did not show it. 'Do whatever he tells you', she said to the servants. What happened next is, in many ways, the most baffling of our Lord's miracles. In spite of the ingenious attempts of embarrassed interpreters, it is impossible to misunderstand John. He tells us that Jesus had the servants fill six large water pots, used for ritual purification, as well as for the obvious purpose of washing the dust off the feet of guests. From this large supply of water, Jesus furnished the wedding with wine, which the steward of the feast commended as being better than the stuff they had consumed earlier. It was not generally known at the feast what had happened, though the servants who drew the water knew, as did the disciples. John tells us that the event manifested the glory of Jesus and that, as a result, 'his disciples believed in him'.

Now John clearly wishes us to see various layers of meaning in this event, but, just as clearly, we ought to begin with the simplest explanation. By his action, Jesus saved his host from a major social embarrassment and, according to some commentators, from the possibility of a lawsuit, since there was a strong element of reciprocity in the marriage customs of the Near East. Failure to furnish a wedding with an adequate supply of wine could have led to a heavy financial penalty. So the gift of Jesus was not just a frivolous act of supernatural extravagance. It was a characteristic response to human need. Nevertheless, it was staggering in its prodigality. By his presence and first miracle that he wrought at Cana of Galilee, our Lord affirmed the reality, as well as the wistfulness and vulnerability, of all purely human joy.

Perhaps a wedding feast captures the poignancy of human joy more than anything else. There are two elements that are strongly present on such occasions, Eros and alcohol. Our Lord's presence at Cana can be said to affirm both. Nevertheless, we have already seen in his remarks to his mother that something else is also present, though it is difficult to capture it in words. The word that suggests itself to me is Transcendence. Jesus is present at Cana, but there is a hint of something in his attitude that is apart from the joy of that day; there is just a hint of a strong and grieving separateness; a little edge of sorrow runs through the joy of it. A moment's meditation soon tells us why. God 'knoweth whereof we are made. He remembereth that we are but dust', as Psalm 103 reminds us. He knows our vulnerability, and he knows how love and wine have been used to assuage the pain we have often felt. Erotic love, the longing to lose ourselves in another, the longing for a relationship that, at the same time, both heightens and obliterates our own identity, is a parable of our need for God. But it is more than that, even. It is itself a kind of searching for the Other in the other. There is a terrible loneliness in it, and an awful gentleness, that is never fully satisfied because it never completely finds its object. Evelyn Waugh captures this poignancy perfectly in some words in *Brideshead Revisited*:

> Perhaps all our loves are merely hints and symbols; vagabond-language scrawled on gateposts and paving-stones along the weary road that others have tramped before us; perhaps you and I are types and this sadness which sometimes falls between us springs from disappointment in our search, each straining through and beyond the other, snatching a glimpse now and then of the shadow, which turns the corner always a pace or two ahead of us. (Evelyn Waugh, *Brideshead Revisited*, p. 288).

Alcohol has something of the same character as erotic love. It is a euphoric agent which can help to assuage, for a time, the pains of loneliness and loss which afflict most of us some of the time, and some of us most of the time. I suppose that what we suffer from is an inescapable sense of our transience and vulnerability, the certainty of our own mortality. Something of this gentle and tragic insight was captured by that endearing old melancholic, A. C. Benson, in one of the entries in his voluminous journal:

> The feeling came to me for an instant, that all the world was one. The secret came close . . . out of the air, over the sea . . . and was gone again in an instant. The thought of the death that overhangs the world, that waits for me, clouded my peace for a time . . . the long procession of those who have lived and who sleep . . . calling the world their own for a space, and then disappearing so utterly. What is there behind it all? Why should one love and hope, be full of eagerness, desire, beauty? Only to die and be silent in the dust? (A. C. Benson, quoted in Newsome, *On the Edge of Paradise*, p. 183).

Newman had captured this melancholy truth even more eloquently:

> Man rises to fall, he tends to dissolution from the moment he begins to be; he lives on indeed in his own children, he lives on in his own name, he lives not on in his own person. He is as regards the manifestation of his nature here below, as a bubble that breaks and as water poured out upon the earth. He was young, he is old, he is never young again. This is the lament over him, poured forth in verse by Christian and by heathen. The greatest work of God's hands under the sun, he, in all the manifestations of his complex being, is born only to die. (*Sermons Preached on Various Occasions*, p. 165)

This sense of our own frailty and finitude should induce in us a kind of large-hearted compassion for the more amiable weaknesses of men and women. After all, as Gerard Manley Hopkins knows, 'any comfort serves in a whirlwind'. Our Lord was called a gluttonous man, a wine-bibber and a sinner, one feels, precisely because he understood the longings that lay behind the excessive behaviour of some of his less respectable friends. He knew, we are told, 'what was in man', he knew 'whereof we were made', and, while he never weakly condoned human sinfulness, one senses in him a gentleness towards our frailties, 'as a father pitieth his children'.

And yet, that undeniable note of severity is never absent, either. By his presence and first miracle at Cana, our Lord affirms and in some sense consecrates our search for self-transcendence in love and in the good gifts of the earth he has provided. But that is not enough. It is not where our real joy is to be found.

What is this joy we search for, then, and where is it to be found? When we are wrestling with an abstract and elusive concept, it often helps to look at what is clearly its opposite. In this case, it is Dejection. This word has, from its Latin root, a number of other words with which we are familiar, such as Rejection, such as Projectile. At the root is the meaning 'throw'. To be rejected is to be thrown-out. A projectile is something thrown. Dejection is that state one falls into if one has been thrown out or rejected. Counsellors see dejected people every day of their lives, people who have been rejected by parents or family, people who have been thrown-out, thrown-over, cast away. They are overwhelmed with an enormous sense of loss; they feel like some useless object that has been thrown away because it is no longer of any value; they are cast out and cast down. Such people look 'downcast', as we say; they are dejected. They feel like emotional refuse, and they go through life punishing themselves and others for that awful and original rejection.

But we are all, to some extent, victims of dejection. In some mysterious sense, we are all cast out of a homeland. Existential philosophers have conceptualized this state of feeling. They call it 'thrown-out-ness'. Mysteriously, we feel ourselves to be not quite where we belong. This accounts for our strange preoccupation with the future, with progress, or getting-on or arriving somewhere. There is a restless, questing quality in us that prevents us ever really feeling at home. Something out there is going to come our way. Some people call this preoccupation with the future, hope; but it is, in most cases, a kind of desperate wishful thinking. Many people, many poor people in particular, feel that they are caught in a trap, and that, someday, someone will lift them from it.

We are all in a far country, cut off from a joy we have never known, yet are born, somehow, remembering. Traces, rumours of that joy are all around us in this life, but we never quite possess it. C. S. Lewis is the supreme expositor of this bittersweet longing we all feel. He says:

> The books or the music in which we thought the beauty was located will betray us if we trust to them; it was not *in* them, it only came through them, and what came through them was longing . . . they are not the thing itself: they are only the scent of a flower we have not found, the echo of a tune we have not heard, news from a country we have never yet visited. (*The Weight of Glory*, p. 8).

Yet we go on looking, searching for a beauty and permanence we never find in this life. Have you ever stood before some valley or mountain range or gentle fold of hills, at dawn or sunset, and felt in you a strange hunger, a heart-hunger that is close to sorrow and joy at the same time? Or have you ever watched a sleeping child, and felt your heart turn over with a strange grieving love? These are examples of the longing we have for the beauty which comes through the world, yet which we cannot here and now possess. And it haunts us.

In contrast to all this is true joy. Joy is a complete sense of belonging and trust. The person in whom there is joy has a secure sense of being loved and wanted, of being valued and cherished. With it comes an enormous sense of liberty and strength. You don't have to be constantly searching for reassurance. You are not for ever trying to secure some place, somewhere, because you know you belong, have roots. You are free of care, in a fundamental sense. We see the rich and paradoxical character of joy in the New Testament. The joy that John speaks of, for instance, is what accompanies closeness to Jesus. If the disciples cleave to Jesus, as the branches cleave to the vine, his joy will be in them. Yet this joy coexists with the most wrenching pain. It is the joy, the oneness, which Jesus has with the Father and which he shares with his disciples. At last, all that heart-stopping longing is assuaged. That endless search for the homeland is accomplished. Joy wells up within them, though the rage of the world breaks upon them. This is the joy that was set before Jesus, the Letter to the Hebrews tells us, and for which he endured the cross and despised the shame of it. It is the joy that caught Paul out of himself as he sat in his prison

13

cell in Rome, writing to his beloved Philippians. The old prisoner of the Lord, removed from all earthly joys, deprived even of his old cloak and his precious parchments, calls upon his friends to rejoice! 'Rejoice in the Lord always; again I will say, Rejoice.' We see something of it in the life of John Henry Newman, of whom Wilfrid Ward said: 'His life as a Catholic recalls the device inscribed at the beginning of a Benedictine Prayer Book—the word "Pax" encircled with a crown of thorns' (*Life of Newman*, vol. i., p. 200). Jesus brings his friends joy, joy that the world cannot take from them, but it is a joy that often has to live with what the world understands as complete rejection and loss. Indeed, Paul makes the paradox quite explicit in his letter to the Philippians: 'Whatever gain I had, I counted as loss for the sake of Christ. Indeed I count everything as loss because of the surpassing worth of knowing Christ Jesus my Lord. For his sake I have suffered the loss of all things, and count them as refuse, in order that I may gain Christ and be found in him' (Philippians 3:7–9).

In one sense, then, the Christian gospel can be described as the costly discovery of true joy. What we could not find by searching, but what we caught hints and rumours of, came freely among us. Jesus brought with him, according to John, the *glory* of that place. The hints and suggestions we have found in poetry and music, the hungering that has risen in us as we contemplate great beauty, the sudden, startled moment of awareness of the Unseen in our midst, all these are touched with a sort of fleeting glory, they impart a mysterious sense of hidden majesty, they startle us, as though a sudden call of trumpets had summoned us. Then, alas, the world rolls back into its place and we are left forlorn. As John testifies, however, that glory we hunger for broke upon us in Christ Jesus. Those who drew near to him found that all their longings found answer in him. They 'beheld his glory'.

And at Cana of Galilee that glory flared out in a miracle of compassionate irony. Nothing is simple in John. He learnt from Jesus that all things come in parables. And what we in our confident blindness think to be merely facts, are really symbols, parables of greater realities. We think that we want passion and red burgundy, but the lord of love and the creator of wine knows that they will never satisfy the real longing that drives us. Nevertheless, as I have said, he affirms our dependence on these things and what they

14

represent, he remembers that we are but dust. But there is a divine irony in his provision for us, and John offers us a riddle that we might read it.

The clue lies in that extravagant outpouring of wine which rescued the wedding feast at Cana. When we reach the end of our own resources, we have not reached the end of all possibilities. Indeed, the occasion may provide the living Christ with the opportunity he needs. John wishes us to understand that when all else fails, we can ask for a miracle, and by a miracle he means the power of God in Christ working through the co-operative obedience of men's wills. God, we are to understand, can make a difference, and he can make a dramatic, miraculous difference. He can transform a situation, he can convert a man, he can even renew the Church. He can turn water into wine. Those water pots are usually held to be an oblique reference to the old religion of the Jews, with its alleged cold legalism; water, compared to the rich wine of the Christian faith. Well, I'd rather leave the Jews out of it. We don't have to go so far from home to find an even more convincing analogy. All Christians, and all churches have a chronic tendency to formalize their relationship with Jesus, to stiffen it into an external and superficial conformity; to make it a matter of words or gestures, a sort of cultural style; to make it religion, which is what is left of faith when a living relationship with Jesus dies or is never born. Then we are left with various types of human or natural activity, from which the surprise and power of the supernatural have been excluded. That leaves us with ecclesiasticism, not with the Church which is his living body. It leaves us with religious observances, and not with real discipleship. It leaves us with a tradition which is tepid and lifeless, like lukewarm water, which has no power either to cleanse or refresh us. It is the tragedy of our nature that we are always lapsing back into that state. The drama of church history, as well as the adventure of our own discipleship, is that there is always the possibility of transformation and renewal, and the agent of that transformation is always and only Jesus Christ. Renewal in the Church has only occurred when individuals have turned to Jesus and told him, 'They have no wine', and been prepared to be the instruments of his transforming power. When that happens, though his glory is manifested only to the few, the Church is rescued from its failure and the wedding feast continues.

15

Chapter 3

FAITH

So he came again to Cana in Galilee, where he had made the water wine. And at Capernaum there was an official whose son was ill. When he heard that Jesus had come from Judea to Galilee, he went and begged him to come down and heal his son, for he was at the point of death. Jesus therefore said to him, 'Unless you see signs and wonders you will not believe.' The official said to him, 'Sir come down before my child dies.' Jesus said to him, 'Go; your son will live.' The man believed the word that Jesus spoke to him and went his way. As he was going down, his servants met him and told him that his son was living. So he asked them the hour when he began to mend, and they said to him, 'Yesterday at the seventh hour the fever left him.' The father knew that was the hour when Jesus had said to him, 'Your son will live'; and he himself believed, and all his household. This was now the second sign that Jesus did when he had come from Judea to Galilee.

John 4:46–54

The New Testament tantalizes and intrigues us as much by what it leaves unsaid as by what it tells us. It is filled with the names of men and women who make brief appearances and then disappear, never to be heard of again. One of these cameo roles was filled by a man whose name is not even given, when Jesus came again to Cana of Galilee and healed a sick child from a distance. The text only tells us that a *basilikos*, or royal official, approached Jesus and begged him to come down to Capernaum to heal his young son. We don't know the man's name, though two conjectures have been offered. There are two other occasions in the New Testament when officials of Herod's court are mentioned as following Jesus. Luke

16

tells us, at the beginning of chapter eight, that certain women provided for Jesus from their own means, among them 'Joanna, the wife of Chuza, Herod's steward'. And, at the beginning of chapter thirteen of the Acts of the Apostles, Luke again mentions a member of the Herodian court as being among the prophets in the church at Antioch. Among the group, he tells us, was 'Manaen a member of the court of Herod the tetrarch'. Either identification is possible, though we cannot be certain. John simply tells us that the man, whoever he was, believed, 'and his whole house'.

Cana lay on high ground, about twenty miles from Capernaum, which lay below, on the shores of the lake, so there is an added note of authenticity in the text when the man asks Jesus to 'come down' and heal his son. At first Jesus is fiercely discouraging: 'Unless you see signs and wonders you will not believe'. The use of the plural in the verbs indicates that Jesus was addressing the crowds who surrounded him, eager for a new miracle, as well as the man who had travelled up from Capernaum to press his need. As is usual with John, we must be prepared to uncover depths of meaning below the factual. We have to interpret the parable as well as believe in the miracle. And we need have no doubt of the latter. In order for the event to *mean* something, it must first *be* something. In this case, it is a straightforward work of healing. It is also a parable of faith. The man's trust in the healing word of Jesus, 'Go, your son lives', is a parable of that true faith which is surrender to a divine word. The man's agony and need, 'Sir, come down before my child dies', is a parable of the human need that brings us to the brink of revelation. But before true faith is illustrated, we hear our Lord's sad anger at its counterfeits.

Wherever our Lord went he was surrounded by multitudes who were eager to see his signs and wonders. This same attitude, in a more subtle form, was found among his closest followers. They were all more interested in the effects and consequences of Jesus' power, than in Jesus himself. Even if they did the right thing and pledged their faith, they invariably did it for the wrong reason. There is a lot of evidence that most of his apostles followed him because they thought they were hitching their wagons to a star. They were not fundamentally fascinated by *his* glory; they were enraptured by the prospect of seeing themselves reflected in the glory that was his. Their relationship with Jesus simply became a new vessel for their

17

old egotism. It is still the fundamental problem of faith, and it can take many forms.

At its most obvious level, this kind of response to Jesus is really too crass to be dangerous. We might classify it, 'Religion as entertainment'. They follow Jesus because they see signs and wonders. Many people suffer from a profound boredom in life. Often, this is because they lack the persistence and determination which are necessary for acquiring habits and interests that will help them redeem the time that lies so heavily upon them. Their passivity and inertia need to be constantly stimulated. Before the invention of the modern entertainment industry religion fulfilled this role and, in some situations, it still can. Any evangelist knows that he may have to use show business techniques to gain a hearing, but he also knows that, beyond all the hoopla, there must be an individual encounter with God. There will always be those who come for the show, and steadfastly refuse the encounter. This is still one of the dangers of mass evangelism techniques. They can create a need for a constant supply of emotional gratification. Unless they see signs and feel wonderful, they will not believe. Jesus always addressed men and women individually. He deeply suspected the power and self-delusion of men in the mass. He knew how easily their hosannas could turn to shouts of 'Crucify him'. Father Dolling, an evangelist who was never afraid to use entertainment techniques to bring men and women to Christ, once remarked that 'the only way to win men in masses is to hook individuals'. Francis Thompson warned us,

> There is no expeditious road
> to pack and label men for God
> and save them by the barrel-load.

This holds true whether we are trying to attract the masses with Mozart or with bongo drums. There is a type of adherence to the Church that is not faith, though it may be putative faith. It is not yet full, personal surrender. It may be stimulated by the Church's worship or intrigued by its teaching, but it is not yet converted or committed, though it may have occasional bouts of emotional fervour. Every parish priest knows this problem. There are many people in our churches who are permanently stuck into a kind of near-belief. Indeed, if we are honest with ourselves, many of us who live by the gospel are in a similar state.

18

It is possible, after all, to become a religious professional, a servant of the ecclesiastical institution, while holding back from a fully committed surrender to Jesus Christ. There have always been those who have been attracted to the movement started by Jesus, not by the vulgarity of signs and wonders (they may well doubt the authenticity of these, anyway), but by a strange fascination with the structures of faith. Like the apostles, they go after Jesus because there is something in it for them. They may have wandered into the professional study of religion. They may find themselves attracted to the pastoral work of the Church. They may be fascinated by the cultic side of Catholic Christianity. It is possible to follow all these callings with reasonable efficiency, without ever really submitting one's life to the authority and direction of Christ. The problem that faces us is how to transform these types of nominal allegiance into real commitment.

There are some fortunate people in every generation who arrive at real faith by a sort of tranquil ease. William James called them 'once-born types'. I have known several. By some tranquil operation of the divine providence, they simply find themselves believing with total trust. I suppose that the outstanding biblical example of this kind of humble surrender is our Lady. It goes without saying, of course, that the apparent effortlessness of the surrender is far from guaranteeing the absence of suffering. A sword pierced our Lady's heart. The good are not immune from pain. They simply make less fuss than the rest of us.

For most of us, however, faith usually follows some crisis that shocks us into attention. John exemplifies this in the story of the official whose little son is at the point of death. There is something complacent and inattentive about most of us, and we have to be brought to a moment of tragic clarity before we will believe. We have to be brought to a limit, a frontier of loss, before finding the desperation that is the prelude to faith. This is clearly what happened to the man who confronted Jesus on that day in Cana. He had reached the end of all false self-assertion. He did not interrogate Jesus or object to the way he had dismissed him as a seeker after supernatural thrills. By this time he was emptied of all egotism. He had come to the end. All that was left was the persistence of desperation: 'Sir, come down before my child dies'.

This desperate supplication is not itself faith, but it is the prelude

19

to faith. Faith itself is a miracle. Whatever crisis it is that brings us to the brink, part of the content of the crisis is an awareness that we have come to a place where no further action by us is possible. It is this very helplessness that defines the crisis. It may be an intellectual crisis, which has brought us to a point where we recognize we have gone as far as our mind will take us in search of meaning, and it has brought us right up to a great abyss. It may be a moral crisis, wherein we confront for the first time the real truth about ourselves, and discover that we have no power to help ourselves. It may be that we are overwhelmed by the tragedy of a terrible loss that has left us stunned and helpless. Whatever the nature of the crisis is, it has served to disarm us completely. It has pulled down our vanity. It has brought us to a frontier which we cannot pass.

There is no point in pretending that what happens next is automatic. I have said that faith, when it comes, is a miracle, but it does not always come. Some remain stranded at that bleak cliff edge for years, aware only of the silence of God. Others hear the answering word from God fast upon their cry of longing. When it comes, however, it always comes as an authoritative word that calls for surrender and submission, and it always comes from outside the self, when we have exhausted the possibilities of the self: 'Go thy way; thy son liveth'. The man, we are told, 'believed the word that Jesus had spoken unto him, and he went his way'. He did not ask for verification. He submitted to the word he had heard, and went his way. And this is a crucial aspect of faith: it is, above all, a form of obedience or submission to a revealed word. This is why faith is often difficult for the clever or successful. It is also why, in the New Testament, it is the poor and the needy who so often answer the word of Christ and who are filled with faith, while the rich are sent empty away. Only the empty cup is filled.

This means that we have to submit to learning a new lesson, we have to learn to live all over again. As Bishop Charles Gore put it,

To become a believer is to submit one's intelligence to learn a new lesson, to study Christ; it is to yield one's self to a 'form of teaching' (Romans 6:17) in order to have one's life refashioned in marked contrast to old and abandoned ways of life; it is to imbibe a new principle in the heart of one's rational being, 'to be

20

renewed in the spirit of one's mind' (Ephesians 4:23); it is to put on deliberately, as a man puts on clothing, a new manhood, Christ's manhood, which is 'according to God' (Ephesians 4:24), that is, based on His own life, and is His 'new creation' in righteousness and holiness (Commentary on Ephesians, p. 181).

This is peculiarly difficult for us today, because of the ascendance of critical rationalism in our culture. We live in an atmosphere which militates against humble submission to any authority, including the authority of God.

One hundred years ago Cardinal Newman foresaw the triumph of this spirit in the Church. When he was made a cardinal, at the end of his long life, he uttered a remarkable prophecy. He warned the Church that the greatest danger which faced it was an ascendant liberalism in theology, which would, in time, erode the distinctiveness and truth of the Christian Faith.

Liberalism in religion [he said] is the doctrine that there is no positive truth in religion, but that one creed is as good as another, and this is the teaching that is gaining substance and force daily. It is inconsistent with any recognition of any religion as true. It teaches that all are to be tolerated, for all are matters of opinion. Revealed religion is not a truth, but a sentiment and a taste; not an objective fact, not miraculous; and it is the right of each individual to make it say just what strikes his fancy.

He had expounded the same thought earlier, in his *Apologia*. Then he had written:

Whenever men are able to act at all, there is the chance of extreme and intemperate action; and therefore, when there is exercise of mind, there is the chance of wayward or mistaken exercise. Liberty of thought is in itself a good; but it gives an opening to false liberty. Now by Liberalism I mean false liberty of thought, or the exercise of thought upon matters, in which, from the constitution of the human mind, thought cannot be brought to any successful issue, and therefore is out of place. Among such matters are first principles of whatever kind; and of these the most sacred and momentous are especially to be reckoned the truths of Revelation. Liberalism then is the mistake of subjecting to human judgment those revealed doctrines which are in their nature beyond and independent of it, and of claiming to determine on intrinsic grounds the truth and value of propositions which rest for their reception simply on the external authority of the Divine Word (*Apologia pro Vita Sua*, p. 288).

The opposite of Liberalism was, according to Newman, obedience to an authoritative source of truth. The man under authority waited upon orders, waited for a word from beyond the undisciplined self. Like the royal official from Capernaum, he waits to hear the divine word and, having heard it, he obeys. For Newman, John Keble was the supreme exemplar, among his Oxford contemporaries, of this spirit of obedience. He says of Keble,

Keble was young in years, when he became a University celebrity, and younger in mind. He had the purity and simplicity of a child. He was a man who guided himself and formed his judgments, not by process of reason, by inquiry or by argument, but, to use the word in a broad sense, by authority. It seemed to me as if he ever felt happier, when he could speak or act under some such primary or external sanction; and could use argument mainly as a means of recommending or explaining what had claims on his reception prior to proof. What he hated instinctively was heresy, insubordination, resistance to things established, claims of independence, disloyalty, innovation, a critical, censorious spirit (Op. cit., p. 289).

The faith of Keble and Newman was grounded as much in love of people as in love of revealed truth. The Christian tradition was primarily a way of salvation for men and women, not a set of abstractions for dons to discuss. When they guarded the faith once delivered to the Church, they believed they were guarding the very Spirit of liberty itself, since the Church was instinct with his life. The grounds on which they opposed the liberal undermining of the faith were as much pastoral as theological. Not only were the liberals wrong about the faith, they were also stealing the children's bread from them, by constantly diverting the attention of the Church from its proper object. Arnold Toynbee has said that it is the fate of the intelligentsia to be permanently unhappy. What is just as true is that they spread their unhappiness around them, by their constant assaults upon tradition. In Newman's words, their 'insubordination,

22

resistance to things established, claims of independence, disloyalty, innovation, critical, censorious spirit', keep the neighbourhood in a permanent uproar. The neighbourhood, of course, can be any institution, from the British Labour Party to the Holy Catholic Church. It is the paradox of this kind of mind, that it is frequently bound into a dogmatic rigidity of its own, yet it operates in an essentially negative way, subjecting its chosen target to an endless critical evaluation. Nothing is left alone. Nothing goes unquestioned. There is, however, no real desire for answers, since accepting answers always involves a form of assent or submission. This kind of mind is fundamentally at odds with the mind of faith. It is essentially reactive, finding its permanent identity in opposition. It is what Peter Berger calls 'the homeless mind', but it is homeless because it is in a state of revolt against permanence.

In contrast, there is a profound conservatism at the heart of all simple religion, and Christianity has always understood it. The common people heard Jesus gladly, whereas the intelligentsia disputed his every claim. I am struggling to acknowledge the primacy of what is simply *given* to us to believe and to follow, before we ever start arguing about it and worrying at it with our reason. We must first of all find ourselves with ground under our feet, before we can even begin to start asking questions about how we got there. With Paul we must stand somewhere. The alternative to this is not freedom or tolerance, but a sort of black hole which sucks us away into weightless oblivion. It was the genius of Newman and Keble, and Gore in a later generation, that they saw, with absolute clarity, mankind's need of this kind of stability, before anything else was even to be thought of. They were committed to this, because they knew that nothing could be built on nothing. They knew that, in order to build, they had to find ground, and that ground had to be *there* before their minds had proved or questioned its reality. There had to be something they could stand on, something that was prior to their own thinking. Life was for action, and to act you had to assume certain things, and that assumption was a kind of faith.

As I write this, I realize more clearly than ever how difficult it is to get this insight into words. Words are the expression of thought, and the event I'm talking about is before thought, or transcends thought; is the ground on which thought itself is able to act. There is a kind of ultimate scepticism about everything that really is a

23

destructive obsession. *We* may not carry it as far as that, but it seriously affects and modifies our attitudes to many things. It creates the soft mind which can decide on nothing, except its disapproval of the hard mind. It is a fact, however, that Anglicanism, in particular, has always had a tenderness for the soft mind. Something of Cranmer's chronic indecisiveness and hatred of false certainty entered the Anglican bloodstream at the very beginning. Indeed, it was probably there in the English genius before the Reformation. There is a permanent family quarrel within the Anglican Church over the very nature of the faith committed to it.

Historically, Anglicans have straddled the divide between what John Macquarrie, following Tillich, calls the Catholic substance and the Protestant principle. The Catholic substance is primary, the very ground of the faith, the truth revealed from heaven. But we possess that treasure in earthen vessels. It has been mediated through the vicissitudes of history and the fallibility of human minds. As Catholics, we will, nevertheless, always and properly, emphasize the authority, the sheer givenness of the faith. Here we have chosen to stand. We know that reason cannot give a final account of this revealed truth. It depends, finally, upon the authority of a divine word. Unless that ground is established, there is nothing left to debate. The truth authenticates itself, as Karl Barth, among others, has cogently argued in our time. It calls forth a response of obedience from our hearts. We commit ourselves to it. It is, by its very nature, miraculous. It comes by revelation. It convinces and convicts by its own authority. It is, of course, 'proved' by its fruits, by the consistency and power of its account of the human predicament. But that 'proving' always follows the act of surrender, it is never the ground of the act of faith. There is an unavoidable leap out into the darkness, before the ledge is found. This is the primordial act of faith. In Gore's words, which I have already quoted: 'to become a believer is to submit one's intelligence to learn a new lesson, to study Christ; it is to yield one's self to a "form of teaching" in order to have one's life refashioned'.

Nevertheless, there has always been another kind of mind within the Church, however unrepresentative of the whole. This is the kind of mind that sees the snags in things. It focuses its attention upon the discrepancies, the historical dubieties, the human tendency to get things wrong. This, above all, is the approach of the supremely

24

rational. They erect a protest against every human institution. They are the permanent opposition, gadflies that buzz round the heads of practical people who want to get things done. They are a permanent necessity, though they are often a frightful bore. The best that can be said of them is that they have often helped to keep the rest of us honest. The worst that can be said is that they often hinder the very movement of life, they obstruct necessary action, by their passion for constant self-examination. They are rarely builders themselves, though they may prove useful in pointing out dangerous flaws in other men's work. In the last analysis, however, they are severely limited in their usefulness. Protest movements are essentially negative, and there are times when something must be done.

The protest mood has become something of a permanent pathology in our world, and it has seriously complicated the work of leaders in any institution. Part of the difficulty lies in the ability of the communications media to inflate protest beyond its proper limits into a permanent counter-institution. It is in the very nature of the publicity media to dwell disproportionately upon protest and negation. Only this is news. So what has always been a necessary corrective to human arrogance and fallibility, has now become something of an end in itself. It is absolutely necessary to have brakes in a car, but cars are made to be driven: they are not made for the sake of the manufacturers of brake blocks. This colossal inversion of roles has tragically affected every authoritative institution in our culture. The insatiable appetite of the news media for publicizable events, and the insatiable vanity of human beings, have joined to create a type of person who is in a constant state of uproar. Institutionalized indignation has an addictive quality which, ironically, flattens rational discourse. So, the very process which began as an assertion of reason against authority, ends by being profoundly anti-rational.

This protest mode has profoundly affected the Church. The Church is always, by virtue of its existence in the world, subject to the pressures of the age. Indeed, it used to be one of the functions of rational protest to remind the Church of that fact. Today, however, the Church is in danger of being kept in a permanent state of uproar, because each scream of protest in the secular sphere is soon

25

transposed into an ecclesiastical register, and the banners are raised, yet again, in the house of God.

All of this has had a profound effect upon the peace of the Church. It has placed the quiet and more reflective type of discipleship at a discount, while noisy activism everywhere prevails. The tragedy in all this is that activists and contemplatives need each other, if they are to avoid the traps they dig for themselves. In the clamour of today's Church, however, the balance has been tragically, perhaps permanently, destroyed. Just as the devouring curiosity of the publicity media has destroyed the ordinary processes of politics, so has it greatly complicated the Church's attempt to find and be obedient to the mind of Christ. However, though these tensions are heightened by the modern passion for protest and display, they have always been present in the Church, and they are probably irresolvable.

Bishop Gore's response to this tension in the Church was to develop a theology of Catholic moderation. For Gore, the ideal of the Anglican Church was that of 'moderate government'. It would allow large differences in teaching and practice, but the differences would exist on a basis of agreement which was definite and deep enough to secure real unity. He was proud of Anglican moderation. It was impossible to examine the ideals of Christ and the apostles without seeing that there might very easily be too much government in the Church, too much theological and moral direction, too high a moral value set on the virtue of mere obedience to external authority. But, if any real government or discipline were to be achieved lines had to be drawn somewhere. In a letter to E. S. Talbot he wrote:

I want to say a word about what you call Rigidity and 'drawing lines'. Surely one real function of the Church is to draw lines. If the Church is wisely liberal, it will draw lines as seldom as possible. But if it is at all true to its traditions and apostolic precedents, it must always appear as a body knowing it has an essential programme to preserve and therefore 'drawing lines' where this treasure is in danger of being invaded. I am quite sure [he went on] that our doubters and seekers are much more likely to be won, if they feel clearly what it is we stand for. It is certainly my experience that men who are outside do not come inside

26

without an act of 'repentance', at least intellectual repentance. They come to an end of their own resources. They must 'believe the Gospel'. Let us by all means keep our Gospel free of encumbrances. But let us hold out unflinchingly our essential message.

It seems quite obvious to me that Gore was right. There is a strange kind of perception abroad that all limits and distinctions are oppressive. There is something in all of us which resists the drawing of limits and the setting of boundaries. This resistance is usually offered in the name of freedom, but it really has its roots in our capacity for arrogant irrationality. The paradox of freedom lies in the fact that it is only really experienced within a clearly defined context. Our experience of games illustrates this. Games excite and compel us, precisely because they operate within strict rules. Because there is a white line round a football pitch and a severe restriction on handling the ball, football is a game which lends itself to an enormously intricate display of controlled and disciplined freedom. The same is true of any other game. The boundaries, the rules, define the game. The same rule applies in our relationships with human beings. There are limits which define and create our freedom. Every sane society, for instance, limits allowable sexual relationships. When the limits are removed we do not experience greater freedom, but profound bondage and fear. The mystery of freedom lies at the heart of the human predicament. There is something in our nature that resists the limits of our reality, which perceives these limits as oppressive; and because political oppression is one of the undoubted facts of human experience, a certain kind of associational fraud occurs, in which genuine outrage at improper discrimination is used as a cover for attacking legitimate discrimination. The recognition that some boundaries are immoral is used to attack the very concept of limits and boundaries as such. This is undoubtedly one element in what traditional theology has thought of as the Fall of Man. There is in all of us an irrational desire to reject the discipline and logic of real human development, in the name of effortless instancy. Our culture is full of examples: art without the mastery of technique; education without the pains of learning; religion without self-denial, without the cross. All of these counterfeits are based upon a rejection of the boundaries that define

27

the very values we claim to be seeking. We listen to the voice of the serpent, as he promises us enlightment without struggle and obedience: 'Ye shall be as Gods'.

The fault lies in a fundamental narcissism in human nature. We are so in love with ourselves that we cannot submit to the demands of the other in our midst. We really believe only in our own reality, with everything else in the wide universe as a stage-set for the little drama in which we star. As a matter of fact, the conventions of television serial drama have created a new kind of consciousness which has fictionalized reality. Our television culture has caused a new kind of self-awareness among people. Life becomes a sort of theatre in which we are constantly observing ourselves. This accounts for much of the display side of public behaviour today, but it also accounts for the tragic breakdown in relationships, notably in marriage. Our main perception is of *ourselves*. Others, unless they play to our role, are experienced as a threat or as a limitation upon our own performance. When the situation becomes uncomfortable, we simply tear up the script and hire a new supporting cast.

Now the whole genius of revealed religion is precisely counter to this prevailing narcissism. It asks us to turn round from gazing upon ourselves and look away from ourselves at what God shows us. In Gore's words, it requires an act of 'intellectual repentance', a change of mind, an act of obedience. This repentance or conversion has to operate on many levels, but it begins with a primary act of acknowledgement. We recognize something out there which exists gloriously in its own right, and not simply as a reflection or aspect of ourselves. Something of this order is already present in the various operating assumptions that undergird our use of reason. We have to accept the validity of our reason as an instrument for apprehending reality. We have to assume it, allow it, let it be the case. No progress is otherwise possible. We cannot wait everlastingly for a proof. We have to believe before we can go on to understand.

The role of revelation in religion has a like, though far greater, primacy. We may reject it after a reasonable investigation. We may debate about its secondary characteristics. What we cannot do, logically, is conform its otherness, its sheer givenness, to our own private preferences, either morally or intellectually. Its limits have to be respected by us, because it is defined by its limits. We may

28

reject it. We cannot say, 'I'll accept you, only if you'll be what I say.' The whole point of the gospel is that it offers us a way, however painful, narrow and dark in places, out of our own predicament. We simply reverse the process, if we start conforming the gospel to the very predicament it is meant to rescue us from. Like the man who came to Jesus at Cana, we find salvation at the end of our resources, not by means of them. Christ was insistent upon this, in his recognition that it was really only the poor and the desperate who would lay hold of the word of life, because only they recognized their need.

After all legitimate allowances are made for the role of reason and argument and protest in religion, therefore, we reach a fundamental point where an act of surrender is required. We must submit, finally, or, with the rich, go empty away.

Chapter 4

RESTORATION

After this there was a feast of the Jews, and Jesus went up to
Jerusalem. Now there is in Jerusalem by the Sheep Gate a pool,
in Hebrew called Bethzatha, which has five porticoes. In these
lay a multitude of invalids, blind, lame, paralysed. One man was
there who had been ill for thirty-eight years. When Jesus saw him
and knew that he had been lying there a long time, he said to
him, 'Do you want to be healed?' The sick man answered him,
'Sir, I have no man to put me into the pool when the water is
troubled, and while I am going another steps down before me.'
Jesus said to him, 'Rise, take up your pallet, and walk.' And at
once the man was healed, and he took up his pallet and walked.

John 5:1–9

There are several possible locations for the pool mentioned in this
passage. It was clearly a pool whose healing properties were associated with some sort of disturbance of the water. An ancient
insertion in the text, after verse three, tells that the sick lay there,
'waiting for the moving of the water; for an angel of the Lord went
down at certain seasons into the pool, and troubled the water;
whoever stepped in first after the troubling of the water was healed
of whatever disease he had.' These conditions could be met by twin
pools at the north-west corner or twin pools at the north-east corner
of the city. Many commentators favour the latter, known as the
Twin Pools at St Anne's, where the remains of arches and 'porticoes'
have been discovered. The identification of the pool with St Anne's
seems to be ancient, for a Crusader church built over the pool has
a mural depicting an angel arising out of the pool. Both of these
sets of pools were probably 'disturbed' by the emptying out of
washings from the temple, which was only about one hundred yards

away. However, there are two other possible locations, both south of the temple, where the disturbing of the water would be accounted for by the bubbling up of a natural spring. One of these pools on the south, the Virgin's Well or 'Gihon' (meaning 'the Gusher'), still has a reputation for healing disease.

Whatever the location might have been, it was clearly the scene of one of the most common and pathetic sights in the ancient world: the constant search for healing by the chronically sick. Wherever our Lord went he seemed to be surrounded by the sick and their relatives. Then, as now, the gravely ill and their families went anywhere and to anyone in their search for new life. This pool had a reputation for healing, albeit with a cruel twist. The sick would be brought by their relatives and friends to lie in porches or colonnades which had been built round the pool, waiting for the disturbance of the water because of emissions from the temple or because the natural spring started gushing. Healing was obviously associated with the first rush of water into the pool, so there must have been something approaching a stampede to get in first. John tells us that 'a multitude of invalids, blind, lame, paralysed' lay in the porticoes. Few of them could have had any expectation of getting into the water on time. One of the unlucky ones, we read, had been paralysed for thirty-eight years. The man was probably brought to the pool every day. He lay there more from habit than in hope. There is something pathetic and self-pitying about him. He speaks in a whining, helpless, hopeless tone of voice. He has withered and atrophied, lost all sense of expectation. He has been beaten by life, and he may even, by now, be getting melancholy satisfaction from his predicament, as he meditates upon his inability to alter his situation for the better. 'Sir, I have no man to put me into the pool when the water is troubled, and while I am going another steps down before me.'

Is there a suggestion of hysterical paralysis in his condition, a measure of self-inflicted injury? Certainly our Lord, in a subsequent encounter, makes a connection between his condition and sin, a connection he does not always make. 'Afterward, Jesus found him in the temple, and said to him, "See, you are well! Sin no more, that nothing worse befall you." ' (verse 14). Whatever the precise nature of the condition was, he responded instantly to our Lord's command. Ignoring the pool, he took up his mat and walked.

John clearly wants us to interpret this encounter between Jesus and the paralytic as more than a straightforward healing story. It is a parable of the human condition, a sign we must read aright. It is a word addressed to us, about our condition. William Temple, in his meditation on this miracle, applied it to the individual's encounter with Jesus. He says, 'When we first come to Him we are not fresh and unspoilt. Some quality of excellence—of strength or influence or natural charm—which was part of God's endowment of our nature, has already been damaged by our worldliness, selfishness or sensuality. And we cannot ourselves restore what is so lost' (*Readings in St John's Gospel*, page 34).

We can, I think, see a progression in the themes and ideas behind John's miracle stories. At the wedding in Cana at Galilee, Jesus is shown to be the source of real joy. He is what we are longing for. But the second miracle at Cana shows us that we do not find this joy by a process of deductive inevitability, like shopping for the item that comes with the best guarantee of performance. Before we can enter into communion with him who is our joy and heart's desire, we must submit to an act of trusting surrender. Presumably this act of faith varies from person to person. Nevertheless, each person is called upon to take a leap that cannot be proved in advance, and something in our nature resists that act of submission. The third miracle at the pool of Bethzatha confronts us with the paradox of our nature. We suffer from a derangement, an ambivalence in our will, the executive side of our nature. In fact, we suffer from a kind of moral and spiritual paralysis. Like the man at the pool, we often know what we ought to do but cannot find the will to do it. Our problem is not a problem of knowledge, of knowing what to do. It is a problem of power, of finding how to do what we already know we ought to do. This miracle makes us face the realities and dilemmas of human sinfulness. The old evangelical name for this process is 'conviction of sin'.

For generations thinkers have produced countless theories to account for the fact of sin and the strange and tragic history of humanity, as well as for individual and social unhappiness. Theories abound which account for human misery, and most of them go on to prescribe remedies. Human misery has been blamed on political and economic structures. It has been blamed on early nurture. It has been blamed on repression, particularly sexual repression. All

32

of these theories have one thing in common: they externalize the problem, they project it onto some outside agent, they put the blame, essentially, elsewhere: 'An enemy hath done this'. And they offer remedies that reflect the elements of their diagnosis. If misery is largely caused by the wrong political and economic structures, then happiness will be found only when they have been radically changed. If misery in adults is caused mainly by the stresses of improper nurturing, possibly even by the tensions and anxieties of the mother affecting the emotional nature of the child in the womb, then the answer must lie in paying greater attention to appropriate methods of infant and child care. If it is believed that misery is really caused by guilt and repression, then the way to create social and private happiness is by following our desires, not by repressing them. Each of these attempts to explain the existence of human misery is a sort of myth of origins, and each has its own power and usefulness. Nevertheless, as with every attempt to produce a comprehensive explanation of human unhappiness, they confuse causes with effects, and leave the real source of misery unhampered. What no one denies is that there is a problem. There is something profoundly amiss with human nature. The great French existentialist, Camus, talks about the Fall, about some profound alienation in our nature, some quality of lost innocence, some sense that we have been driven from a homeland and wander through history, seeking a way to return. The atheist poet, A. E. Housman, captured the same note when he said,

> The troubles of our proud and angry dust
> Are from eternity, and shall not fail.

Humanity's religious traditions account for our present state in a series of myths of the Fall. The instinctive core in most of them attributes the origin of human misery to some act of primal disobedience, some breaking of bounds or overreaching of legitimate limits. So evil is the result of a false desire of independence in us. We refuse to abide by the rules that make the game what it is, so the joy of the game becomes something more deadly and earnest. We will not accept the steps that make the dance, so the delight of the dance is lost in the fear and disorder of growing frenzy.

But there is another element in the great myths of the Fall. There is another agent at work. Rebellion, somehow, had been in the

33

universe before us. Paul calls the source of this rebellion 'the prince of the power of the air'. There are other unseen rebel wills in the universe, and they organize and give a certain coherence and continuity to evil in the world. So there arises a kingdom of evil over and against the Kingdom of God. And those who will not surrender themselves to God become, perforce, servants of this other kingdom.

It is impossible to give a strictly empirical account of this tragic situation. The reality can only be conveyed in metaphor and poem, but our experience of human misery is empirical enough. Jesus offers us no explanation. He takes the situation for granted, largely, I suspect, because he was more interested in changing human nature than in offering an account of it. Without wishing to over-systematize the complex fact of human sinfulness, I would like to suggest that there are three phases or modes of sin, which twine together into a well-nigh unbreakable rope.

We each suffer from an intrinsic flaw in our nature, a chronic derangement of consciousness. Each of us is tragically centred in our own ego. We are born with a tragic bias towards ourselves, which confuses and often vitiates our relationships with others at every level. Or, to change the metaphor, there is a strange magnetic force in each of us which pulls reality in our direction, making us conscious of ourselves as the centre of the universe, the main actor in life's drama. This is obviously true physically. William Temple called this the parable of perspective. We unavoidably experience ourselves as the physical centre of the universe, round which everything else revolves. Tragically, this is true morally and spiritually, as well as spatially. History is the record of the collision of all these egos. An inescapable element in the disorder is the blindness to the real nature of the self which accompanies it. We have enormous clarity when it comes to discerning the faults of others. We are almost blind when it comes to discerning our own.

This is why Jesus spent a lot of time trying to shock people into a real awareness of their condition. Alcoholics are masters at this kind of self-delusion. They adopt innumerable psychological ruses to keep themselves from facing the reality of their situation. Healing begins at the moment they face the truth about themselves with complete honesty. That, too, is a parable of the universal human condition. We constantly delude ourselves, but there can be no health for us till we recognize our own disease. We suffer from

34

ourselves, and part of the tragedy is that we are blind to our own condition most of the time.

But there is a further element in the complex. Not only do we inherit a basic human disposition to selfishness, a warp or bias in our nature; that inherited flaw is particularized by our own precise background. We are all born into a particular context, born into families and societies that are themselves moulded in some sense by the whole entail of the past. So Original Sin has been individualized, personalized, like a modern cheque-book. Each tribe and nation has made sin peculiarly its own. Any counsellor or social worker knows how profoundly modified we are by our background, and they know how difficult it is to break the mould that has enclosed us; they know how difficult it is for us to make what they call, in their jargon, 'developmental changes'.

I am not saying that we come to maturity completely programmed, like a computer. There is always a frail flame of freedom burning somewhere inside us, but our nature has been profoundly modified and distorted by the great force behind us. Fr Kelly, founder of the Society of the Sacred Mission, used to say that you could trace the origins of the First World War back to the building of the Great Wall of China, two millennia before. We are all bound together in a great web of guilt and destiny which affects our every action. This is why the great novelists make better theologians and historians than the professionals. They feel an enormous compassion for, and share an identification with, all those prisoners of time as they work out their tiny, yet tragic destinies. They are somehow touched by the grief of God as he watches and weeps over his ruined creation.

And there's a third phase in the great drama of the Fall. Each of us makes it his own. We add our contribution, our pennyworth, to this vast and increasing debt, by the way we have actually lived; by the things we have done and left undone; by our crying sins and our whispering sins; by our wilful sins and the sins we have concealed, even from our own conscience. We make sin our own by the way we have actually lived. So we arrive, finally, at the state acutely described by St Paul:

> I do not understand my own actions. For I do not do what I want, but I do the very thing I hate. Now if I do what I want,

I agree that the law is good. So then it is no longer I that do it, but sin which dwells within me. For I know that nothing good dwells within me, that is, in my flesh. I can will what is right, but I cannot do it. For I do not do the good I want, but the evil I do not want is what I do. Now if I do what I do not want, it is no longer I that do it, but sin which dwells within me. So I find it to be a law that when I want to do right, evil lies close at hand. For I delight in the law of God, in my inmost self, but I see in my members another law at war with the law of my mind and making me captive to the law of sin which dwells in my members. Wretched man that I am! Who will deliver me from this body of death? (Romans 7:15–24).

God's answer to Paul's tormented question is Jesus Christ. The deliverance that comes in Jesus Christ has two phases, though they are not always experienced in the same order. Part of the work of Christ was clearly accusatory or diagnostic. There was considerable redemptive harshness in Jesus. Anger and judgement poured out of him against hypocrisy and pride and dishonesty and cruelty. Part of his mission was to shock people into real awareness of their condition, to warn them of the lateness of the time. Many of his parables are hot with urgency. But the motive for this abrupt and challenging urgency is entirely positive. It is the tough love of the surgeon who knows there is no time to waste, if the dilatory patient is to be restored to health by means of the healing knife. Jesus grieves over our sinfulness, not because it offends *him*, but because it wounds and damages and may destroy *us*. It is his ambition for us that grieves, his longing that we might find real joy and enduring peace. He came to bring us to repentance, to make us see the exceeding sinfulness of sin; not out of a puritanical distaste for us and a contempt for our frailty, but out of love and a great tenderness. There is a terrible sternness in Jesus Christ, but the overwhelming impression he leaves upon us is one of sorrowing love. This is captured most clearly in the tragic glimpse we have of him as he weeps over Jerusalem, because it knew not where to find peace. 'O Jerusalem, Jerusalem, killing the prophets and stoning those who are sent to you! How often would I have gathered your children together as a hen gathers her brood under her wings, and you would not!' (Matthew 23:37).

If part of his work was diagnostic, then, his real purpose was our restoration to health. He came that we might have life, and have it abundantly, John tells us. He came, in fact, to draw us into his life, to attract us by the glory of his nature. The really revolutionary thing about Christianity is the power of Christ to attract men and women into an abiding relationship with him, in which they are slowly transformed after his likeness. The paradox, of course, is that the more they grow into his likeness, the more like themselves they become. And the instrument of this transformation is what Bishop Gore called 'the expulsive power of a new affection'. Only that can work the miracle we need. Sometimes the miracle is instantaneous. There are chosen souls in every generation who meet Christ and, like the man paralysed for thirty-eight years, act immediately upon his word. Their lives are split in two. A sort of developmental miracle takes place. They are never again fundamentally dis-obedient to the vision of promise and glory they have seen. This seems to have been the general expectation of the first Christians. They met Christ. They repented. They were baptized into his life. They became new men and women. Alas, for most of us and, it would appear, for many of them, that does not truly represent what actually happens.

In those earliest days, it was held that sin was an impossibility for the Christian. The Christian was one whose sins had been washed away in baptism and who, thereafter, committed no sin. If they did fall into sin, they were held to be apostate, to have cut themselves off from the fellowship of faith and to be on the way to destruction. But an important distinction must be made here. There are two broad categories of sinful actions. There is, first, what we call grave or deadly sin, sin which is seriously destructive. This includes all serious lapses in the moral life, serious sins against love and one's fellows. There are lists of them in the New Testament in various places, such as Galatians 5:19: 'Sexual immorality, impurity of mind, sensuality, worship of false gods, witchcraft, hatred, quar-relling, jealousy, bad temper, rivalry, factions, party spirit, envy, drunkenness, orgies and things like that'. These sins are all deadly; they not only destroy the health of the individual who engages in them, but they poison the community as well. In the New Testa-ment these sins are simply ruled out: if you are a Christian you do not commit them; if you commit them, you are not a Christian. This is put with great simplicity in the New Testament:

> Christ appeared to take away sins, and in him there is no sin. No one who abides in him sins; no one who sins has either seen him or known him . . . No one born of God commits sin; for God's nature abides in him, and he cannot sin because he is born of God. By this it may be seen who are the children of God, and who are the children of the devil: whoever does not do right is not of God, nor he who does not love his brother (1 John 3:5).

> It is impossible to restore again to repentance those who have once been enlightened, who have tasted the heavenly gift, and have become partakers of the Holy Spirit, and have tasted the goodness of the word of God and the powers of the age to come, if they then commit apostasy, since they crucify the Son of God on their own account and hold him up to contempt (Hebrews 6:4 ff).

Terrible words about a terrible reality, the reality of sin committed by the Christian who knows better, the reality of grave or mortal sin, the sin which kills.

But there is another kind of sin which need not detain us, which is called venial sin, ordinary sin, the petty imperfections that beset us as humans, but which do not seriously distort our nature. The Church has never bothered too much about these: 'Ask God's forgiveness, and forget about them', it says.

What are we to do about the more deadly sins? As we have seen, the early Church simply ruled them out. However, it was soon discovered that Christians were not miraculously immune to deadly sin. Even after baptism and the gift of the Spirit of God, they fell into grave sin, usually to their own intense sorrow and shame. What was to be done about it? From the very earliest years, therefore, the Church developed the discipline of confession. Tertullian, one of the great theologians of the early Church, called this the second plank after shipwreck. We were shipwrecked by our sin. Baptism was the first plank thrown to us, but when we went under again confession was the second plank which was tossed to us.

It had three parts. First of all there had to be genuine *contrition*, genuine sorrow for the sins committed against God's love. Then

38

there had to be *confession* of the sin committed: and this was not a quiet, discreet little whisper to a priest in a corner; it was public confession to the bishop in the presence of the church, for sin was felt to be an offence against the whole family and not just a private matter. After confession there followed *satisfaction*, which involved various things: it might, for instance, involve restitution of something that had been stolen, though it went further than this, to include a whole pattern of amendment in life, and a genuine change and repentance. If this satisfaction was shown over a period, sometimes of years, the bishop would formally pronounce absolution and the sinner was restored to communion and full fellowship with the Church. From the earliest years this discipline was obligatory for all those who had committed major or grave sin.

Then an unfortunate development set in. Alongside this confession of obligation there grew up a voluntary confession of devotion, not for deadly sin, but for venial sin. This gradually developed as a devout practice, a sort of private spiritual discipline, and soon the principle of obligation crept in here as well. By the fourteenth century confession was obligatory for all, whether or not they were in a state of grave sin, and the whole medieval apparatus of confessional discipline was established and became a major instrument of social control. Buried beneath it all lay the important recognition that deadly sin was a serious matter and must be attended to by the Christian.

This was soon forgotten in the great disruption that followed upon the Reformation. The Reformers threw out the whole confessional system, because it had grown corrupt and was being constantly abused, but they jettisoned much that was good as well as much that was bad. It was right to reject the universal obligation to confess, even when there was no deadly sin on the conscience, but it was a real mistake to lose the ancient discipline of obligatory confession for serious sin. The Anglican Reformers retained the ancient practice of confession for grave sin, but they removed its obligatory nature and they tucked it away in the Prayer Book, like a mad relative in an attic. If you wanted to find the form for confession in the old Prayer Book, you had to go to the service for the Visitation of the Sick to find it. Happily, in the new American Prayer Book it has been given appropriate prominence.

Of all the Reformers, Luther's attitude to the sacrament of confession was the most enlightened and refreshing, and I think it would be difficult to better it even today. He retained confession, and had a high view of it, but he stripped it of all its gloomy legalism. It was almost a part of baptism itself, an extension of baptism. In confession, the one baptism for the forgiveness of sins was re-affirmed, reapplied, made real again, felt to be true again, redis-covered. So confession was not really a separate sacrament at all; it was a dynamic and joyous actualizing of the meaning of baptism throughout one's life, a constant bringing of it up to date. It was not a neat and systematic method with three parts, all of which had to be gone through before the whole thing was complete—it was the way in which the Christian freely laid hold upon the joyous reality of Christ's forgiveness, again and again, when necessary.

The great value of Luther's approach is that it allows us to recognize the seriousness of grave sin. It recognizes its corrupting and fatal effects upon the life of the Christian and the Church, and the obligation to do something about it; but it avoids all the ma-nipulation and red tape which surrounded it in the medieval Church.

The Anglican Church has always known the practice of confes-sion, but it was not until the Catholic revival of the nineteenth century that its importance and its positive value were rediscovered. The use of confession became one of the marks of the Christian who was really serious about following Christ. But it was not all gain. There was an indiscriminate takeover of the medieval view that confession was obligatory for everyone, even in the absence of grave sin, so that we returned to the practice of the confession of devotion for the devout few, rather than allowing the confession of obligation to become the norm for all.

There is considerable evidence today that the use of this spiritual discipline is declining, and since there is no evidence of a propor-tionate decrease in sinfulness, it would seem that there is a decline in general moral seriousness among Christians, and an accommo-dation to the low standards of society.

Let me summarize the implications of this brief history. If Christ-ians find themselves in a state of grave sin after a serious moral lapse (no matter how long ago), as opposed to the petty imperfec-tions which beset us daily, then they are obliged, by the most ancient traditions of the Church, to confess those sins through the

40

Church at the earliest opportunity. This is obviously not a legal obligation—there is no one to enforce such a thing—but it is a personal, spiritual obligation; it is an indication of the seriousness of our Christian commitment. The Christian cannot simply sit loosely to the presence of serious moral evil in his life; it is a cancer which must be dealt with if real Christian progress is to be made.

And this is not a frightening and morbid necessity. Rather, it is an enormous and joyous release. We have been given a way by which we can constantly achieve the miracle of moral and spiritual rebirth. We have been offered a means of constant transformation. We have been given a way by which we can enter into the meaning of the resurrection of Christ from the dead, because we can, by going down into the death of our sin and its seriousness, rise again to newness of life. The experience may be painful to a certain degree, but pain is not its main point, any more than the dentist treats us to bring us pain. The pain is often an unavoidable accompaniment of new health and life. Confession is one of the ways in which we meet Jesus and experience his risen life. Like the man at the pool of Bethzatha, we must respond to the offer of Jesus with an urgent act of will. Contrition and confession are the essential preludes to that wonderful release and forgiveness which come in this sacrament. If Christians are labouring under a guilty con-science; if they have succeeded in burying their guilt beneath years of forgetfulness; if they have grown a hard skin of apathy over their souls, then Christ offers them immediate release: 'Do you want to be healed?', he asks, and offers them a powerful and permanent means of transformation.

Chapter 5

COMMUNION

After this Jesus went to the other side of the Sea of Galilee, which is the Sea of Tiberias. And a multitude followed him, because they saw the signs which he did on those who were diseased. Jesus went up into the hills, and there sat down with his disciples. Now the Passover, the feast of the Jews, was at hand. Lifting up his eyes, then, and seeing that a multitude was coming to him, Jesus said to Philip, 'How are we to buy bread, so that these people may eat?' This he said to test him, for he himself knew what he would do. Philip answered him, 'Two hundred denarii would not buy enough bread for each of them to get a little.' One of his disciples, Andrew, Simon Peter's brother, said to him, 'There is a lad here who has five barley loaves and two fish; but what are they among so many?' Jesus said, 'Make the people sit down.' Now there was much grass in the place; so the men sat down, in number about five thousand. Jesus then took the loaves, and when he had given thanks, he distributed them to those who were seated; so also the fish, as much as they wanted. And when they had eaten their fill, he told his disciples, 'Gather up the fragments left over, that nothing may be lost.' So they gathered them up and filled twelve baskets with fragments from the five barley loaves, left by those who had eaten.

John 6:1–13

I have already pointed out that in reflecting upon the seven great signs in John's Gospel we have to do two things. First of all, we have to study the detail of the outward event, the external sign. For us, however, something else is more important: We have to penetrate to the inward meaning; we have to discover *what* is signified. This whole approach, this double perspective, governs all of John's

42

Gospel and what we see there of the response of men and women to Christ. Christ was himself a sign, in this sense. He was a man, but he was a man in whom the fulness of God was veiled. Again and again, John shows us people who stop short at the outward manifestation. They get no further than the compelling humanity of the man who confronted them, either in enthusiasm or in anger. They either want to make him a king, or they want to throw him from a cliff. They never get further than the immediate surface event and its impact upon them. We find a precise example of this in the effect upon the multitude of the great miracle of feeding which Jesus performed.

John tells us in verse twenty-two, that on the day after this great miracle the crowd pursued Jesus to the other side of the sea of Galilee. Jesus did not welcome their enthusiastic pursuit: 'Truly, truly, I say to you, you seek me, not because you saw signs, but because you ate your fill of the loaves' (verse 26). They did not reflect upon the meaning of what had happened, they did not *see* the sign, because they were so intent upon satisfying their perfectly real physical hunger. The Gospel is full of these missed encounters and lost opportunities. It is heavy with the dulness of men and women who do not or will not see what is happening in their midst. John sums up the terrible sense of loss that pervades the ministry of Christ in one poignant verse: 'He came unto his own, and his own received him not' (1:11). Men and women are so heavy with their own needs, so absorbed by their own struggles, so intent upon their own designs that they fail to see the one who stands before them and offers them their heart's desire. In Graham Greene's haunting phrase, they 'miss happiness by seconds at an appointed place'.

The Gospel of John, in a series of vivid and eloquent impressions, captures the drama of God's eternal approach to us and our endless failure to recognize his appearing. 'He was in the world, and the world was made by him, and the world knew him not. He came unto his own, and his own received him not' (1:10–11). And we find the whole tragic theme rehearsed in the story of the feeding of the five thousand and its aftermath. All the great themes of approach and rejection, of failure to see aright what is made plain, are set forth in this narrative. At the same time, John is showing us a more subtle set of connections. He is wanting us to see the essentially

43

parabolic nature of life itself. Everything speaks of God in parables, in hints and whispers, if only we will pay attention long enough to understand.

Characteristically, John places all these layers of meaning in an event which can be met on a purely material or historical level, the miraculous feeding of a multitude of people. As with the miracle at the wedding in Cana, C. S. Lewis points out, the miracle was a short-circuiting or concentrating of a permanent activity of God the creator. As God turns water into wine by an organic process which he short-circuited at Cana, so each year he turns a little corn into much corn; and as the teeming seas multiply their kind according to laws established by God so, 'on that day, at the feeding of the thousands, incarnate God does the same; does close and small, under his human hands, a workman's hands, what he has always been doing'. The point is that men and women respond to both the natural and the supernatural miracle in exactly the same way. They concentrate on *what* happens, not on *who* makes it happen. As we gaze on the world, we stop short at it, obsessed with the production of bread, rarely with him whose gift it is. John wants us to recognize the work of God. He shows us a characteristic drama of human incomprehension. He shows us human beings confronted by an act of divine power, by an overture from God, who find it impossible to make the connection. They do not read the sign. Instead, they search for more bread. 'You seek me, not because you saw signs, but because you ate your fill of the loaves.' In a universe that is a sacrament of the divine presence, we rarely go beyond the tangible. Jesus, however, is a patient teacher. He knows that we need bread, but he uses our need of bread as a parable for something far more important. Our undeniable need for food which perishes is used by him as a way of drawing our attention to deeper needs, which the food of earth cannot satisfy. He did this at the wedding at Cana, drawing our attention to the source of real joy. He did it at the well in Samaria, where he used a woman's thirst for water to remind her of her real but unadmitted thirst for God. And he does it here, this time by using our need for bread as a parable of profounder needs. 'Do not labour for the food which perishes, but for the food which endures to eternal life' (verse 27). In the story of the feeding of the five thousand and in the discourse by our Lord that follows it, John is urging us to recognize two things. Bread is a sign of our need for God. But it is also a symbol of his presence with us.

Unfortunately, the word 'symbol' has lost much of its original power. It comes from the Greek *sumballein*, which is the bringing together of two things which have been separated. One of its uses is to provide an introduction or to supply an identification. If two kings make a secret bond by breaking a ring in two, each keeping a half, a secret emissary from one to the other could identify himself by supplying the other half of the ring. This is a symbol. So, in a sense, is a bridge across a river, which succeeds in bringing both sides together. A symbol, therefore, is not a mere cipher, something which artificially represents something else which is actually absent. Language is a good example. All those signs are meaningless, unless they can be read, unless the mind can connect with them and make meaning. Symbols actually effect something. They bring together what has been broken apart, for whatever reason. Life is full of examples, but life itself seems to be part of a broken symbol. A mysterious sense of loss and incompleteness haunts life. There is something about our experience of life which makes it radically incomplete. We are all, in one way or another, on a search for a mysterious finality, some connecting meaning or purpose that will somehow gather the broken fragments that remain into an enduring and satisfying unity. Religion explains that sense of incompleteness by claiming that we have somehow fallen out of step with reality. We have lost our way in the enchanted wood, and in seeking for what we have lost we become fixated on the creation rather than using it as a means of communion with the creator. That is why the world is so dangerous for us; not because it is wrong in itself, but because we are orphaned, looking for someone to belong to; and fatal substitutes abound. Presumably in an unfallen universe we would have communion with God through all he has created. Nothing would be broken off from God. Now, alas, we live in a universe of broken symbols, and we only ever have half of the truth, half of the joy we seek.

Music is the best example of this strange quest we are on. Music enthralls us because it seems permanently poised on the brink of what we are seeking, yet it never quite brings the broken fragments together. It has us, time after time, on our tip toes, waiting for a footfall that's never heard, for a door to open that remains poignantly shut. Popular music, as well as more enduring folk music, reflects this strange longing and incompleteness, but it is, above all, in great music that we come closest to the unbearable sense of loss that afflicts us. The music of Edward Elgar captures, for me, what I am trying to say. In the Cello Concerto and in the Second Symphony, he captures man's tragedy and grandeur as he seeks to find the meaning of life and history. Elgar and his music are associated with the high point of the British Empire. He caught all the pride and certainty of that brief moment, as well as the agony and pathos of its swift dissolution. His music seems to say that humanity is filled with magnificent longings that history cannot fulfil. Our life is a brilliant series of disappointments, because we wait, poised for a finale that never comes. The thrill of the trumpets lifts and cuts through the air, but they are always blown above our graves, and even as they thrill us they fill us with a sense of loss.

'He was in the world', says John, 'and the world was made through him, yet the world knew him not.' Though it lay there, just below our gaze, we never did find the part of our life's meaning that was mysteriously broken off. So, John tells us, God himself accomplishes for us what we could not do for ourselves. This is the meaning and purpose of Christ. He unites the broken fragments. He makes of the two, one, the divine with the human, the spiritual with the material. And he does this by making the material a vehicle of the spiritual. Jesus himself unlocked the meaning of the riddle of the great miracle of the feeding of the multitude. John gives us our Lord's commentary on the event in the rest of chapter six. John does not give us an account of the last supper, the institution of the Mass. Instead, he gives us this great chapter. He takes the Eucharist for granted. What he wants to do is to make sure we know what it means. In it, we are told, we have communion with the living Christ. At last the material and the spiritual are conjoined. The eucharistic bread is the outward and visible sign of the communion we can truly have with the risen Christ.

And here we must recall John's use of a sign. He does not dismiss the outward event, for two reasons. First of all, God respects our bodies, our materiality. We are not pure spirit, not angels. He comes to us in a mode appropriate to our condition; in something we can touch, see and handle. God in my hands! This was the heart

46

of the message that John was impelled to proclaim. He summarizes it in the opening words of his first letter:

> That which was from the beginning, which we have heard, which we have seen with our eyes, which we have looked upon and touched with our hands, concerning the word of life—the life was made manifest, and we saw it, and testify to it, and proclaim to you the eternal life which was with the Father and was made manifest to us—that which we have seen and heard we proclaim also to you, so that you may have fellowship with us; and our fellowship is with the Father and with his Son Jesus Christ (1 John 1:1–3).

But this coming of God in the flesh is no mere concession to our condition, a children's game to help us grasp a difficult truth. It is a reintegration of God's original creation. In an unfallen universe the material would not be a snare to hold us back from God, but a means of communion with God, because it would be for ever conjoined to God. In Christ and in the Eucharist, God has re-established that original union, he has restored the sacramental nature of the universe. That union is not yet absolutely and transparently achieved, of course, but the Eucharist affirms that it is, even now, being achieved. What had been broken is coming together again. That is the Christian hope, the hope that has sustained millions of Christians down the ages in the face of life's surrenders and disappointments. This hope is not something that is promised but endlessly postponed. We have a taste of that communion now, as we journey. There are three great miracles that proclaim the re-unification of God's divided creation. The incarnation unites our flesh with God. The resurrection takes that flesh and transforms it into its final nature, its eternal form. And the Eucharist is the continuous miracle by which we are brought into the reality of the other two. In the Eucharist we are knit slowly into the mystical life of the incarnate and glorified Christ. Like a fracture that slowly heals, our lives are being knit to his life. And matter is the medium by which that communion is achieved.

The Eucharist, then, partaken of in faith, is the way we grow into Christ. But it is also the sign of another and greater reality. The bread and wine which are transmuted into the very presence of Christ for us, localize and fix for our senses what is happening to the whole creation. The universe is being restored to its original communion with God. In the mysterious and compelling words of Teilhard de Chardin, the Mass is a sign of God's will for the whole creation: 'Step by step it irresistibly invades the universe. It is the fire that sweeps over the heath; the stroke that vibrates through the bronze . . . the sacramental species are formed by the whole of creation, and the duration of creation is the time needed for its consecration' (*The Divine Milieu*, p. 102).

Two consequences follow from this. It points, first of all, to the absolute centrality of the Mass in the Christian tradition. In some ways, of course, this is already recognized. So successful has been the liturgical movement in the Church, that it has established the Eucharist at the centre of parish worship almost everywhere, but at considerable cost. The Eucharist has become a familiar thing, and some of the wonder has been lost. This familiarization has been intensified by the character of many modern rites and the way they are celebrated. The Eucharist is often handled with a casual, almost breezy carelessness today, and it is used as an adjunct of almost any kind of ecclesiastical event. I am not arguing for a remystification of the Mass, but for a true appreciation of it. We are handling the Word of life, the sacramental presence of the living Jesus. We have, in a sense deeper than poetry, God in our hands, yet we can so easily treat his presence with a sort of matey familiarity. Perhaps the old prayer manuals, with their lengthy preparations for Mass and thanksgiving after Mass, overdid it a bit, but they were overdoing an instinct that was entirely appropriate. We need to recover some of the joy and awe our fathers in the faith had, as they fought to have the Mass at the centre of the Church's life.

There is another momentous implication for Christians of this great teaching about the centrality of the Eucharist. It was put with characteristic fervour by Bishop Frank Weston at the second Anglo-Catholic Congress in 1923 when he said:

The one thing England needs to learn is that Christ is in and amid matter, God in flesh, God in Sacrament. If you are prepared to fight for the right of adoring Jesus in His Blessed Sacrament then, when you come out from before your tabernacles, you must walk with Christ, mystically present in you, through the streets of this country, and find the same Christ in the peoples of your

48

cities and villages. You cannot claim to worship Jesus in the tabernacle if you do not pity Jesus in the slum . . . It is folly, it is madness to suppose that you can worship Jesus in the Sacrament and Jesus on the throne of glory when you are sweating him in the bodies and souls of his children . . . You have your mass, you have your altars . . . Now go out into the highways and hedges and look for Jesus in the ragged and the naked, in the oppressed and the sweated, in those who have lost hope and in those who are struggling to make good. Look for Jesus in them; and when you have found him, gird yourself with his towel of fellowship and wash his feet in the person of his brethren.

This is a call we must hear, but it suffers from the great disadvantage that characterizes much pulpit rhetoric. It is a broad and passionate exhortation to Christians to heal the sufferings of the world, but it offers no specific programme of action that might guide them through the complicated maze of human sorrow. It serves, however, to confront us with the great mystery of inequality and the stubborn problem of human poverty. It lays upon Christians an enormous burden of anguish for the sufferings of the mass of humankind. We cannot escape from that anguish. Unfortunately, much pulpit rhetoric stirs up the anguish and piles on the guilt, without pointing to any unarguably obvious solution to the problem. The end for which we must all long and for which we must all work is a world cleansed of injustice and oppression. Unfortunately, there is less clarity and agreement among Christians in finding the means that will achieve that end. How do we deal with the baffling complexity of human suffering? And how do we deal with the fact that Christians are, and always have been, in radical disagreement with each other about the best responses to the problem?

There have been two practical responses to the fact of poverty by Christians. The most Christlike and heroic is also the most rare. It is to become poor. It is to identify oneself totally with the lives of the poor. The motive for this is twofold. It is a work of magnificent compassion, but it is also the result of a desire to be mystically identified with the Christ who told us that he himself was sacramentally present in the poor. The most famous example of this Christlike identification with the poor is, of course, St Francis of Assisi. The most celebrated modern example is Mother Teresa of

49

Calcutta. Other examples abound in Christian history. One thinks, for instance, of the tormented attempt of Simone Weil to identify herself totally with the poor and hungry, to the point of self-annihilation. Vocations to the life of heroic poverty are rare, but they embolden the rest of us to some partial identification with the poor. Baron von Hügel always insisted that any holy lady who came under his spiritual direction had to spend one day a week visiting and helping out in the East End of London. Many today would find his approach patronizing, but it was undoubtedly correct in its recognition that the spiritual life was incomplete without some engagement in the world. It is this incarnational imperative which still sends Christians out to perform works of mercy. Christians are not only the backbone of voluntary organizations for the relief of suffering, they have themselves invented many of the agencies that exist to serve the poor, the mentally ill, those in prison, the despairing and the dying. In these practical ways, countless Christians down the ages have made their private responses to Christ's command to them to meet him in the poor and the needy.

The matter becomes altogether less straightforward when Christians seek to find structural or institutional responses to the problem posed by the existence of human poverty and need. Here Christians must accept a high level of permanent conflict among themselves. In spite of the sweeping generalities that are constantly offered by ideological contestants, there is little evidence that truth is easily discovered in these matters or, when discovered, is easily applied to the complexities of history. Boethius captured the reality of this mysterious discordance in one of his most famous poems, translated by Helen Waddell:

> This discord in the pact of things,
> This endless war twixt truth and truth,
> That singly hold, yet give the lie
> To him who seeks to yoke them both—
> Do the gods know the reason why?
>
> (Helen Waddell, *Mediaeval Latin Lyrics*, p.49)

There are three broad responses to the problem posed for Christians by the existence of evil and suffering in the world, though each response can be indefinitely subdivided. Perhaps the most primitive response is to cut off all ties with society. The world is evil. States,

50

nations and societies are intrinsically corrupt. They are immoral in their relations with each other, and there is no way the Christian can be involved in their affairs without being corrupted. Christians must come out from among them and be apart. They must create the perfect society within the Christian family. Only here is the life of holiness possible. In society it is impossible. Christians, therefore, must withdraw from society as it is organized. In the jargon of sociologists, this leads to the privatization of Christianity. It is often classified as the sectarian or pietist approach. The intriguing thing about it, however, is that it has often led to the purification of society. Examples abound in history of groups who have withdrawn from the world in this way, yet who have profoundly affected the course of history. What Montalembert said of Benedict of Nursia can be broadly applied to many groups and may one day be applied to the Pentecostal churches in South America:

> Historians have vied in praising Benedict's genius and clear-sightedness; they have supposed that he intended to regenerate Europe, to stop the dissolution of society, to prepare the reconstitution of political order, to re-establish public education, and to preserve literature and the arts ... I firmly believe that he never dreamt of regenerating anything but his own soul and those of his brethren the monks (De Montalembert, *The Monks of the West*, vol i, p. 436).

Before dismissing the privatization of Christianity, we ought to remember that the Holy Spirit is extremely versatile in the way he works upon the complexities of human history.

The second response comes from Christians who believe that there is no distinctive Christian approach to these matters. Nations are governed by a lower morality than individuals, the morality of force and compulsion. If Christians are involved in politics they, like everyone else, have to operate within the fallen system of human groups. Christians cannot alter the tragic necessities of history. There are two kingdoms: the Kingdom of God, which is concerned with ultimate values; and the kingdom of Caesar, which operates at a sub-Christian level, governed by the sword, as Paul puts it in the Letter to the Romans. Just as there is no Christian biology or way of building a house, so there is no Christian politics, as such. You have to learn to operate within the necessities of institutional power, by understanding the laws that govern the kingdoms of this world. If you seek to apply private Christian morality to relations between states, you may only make a bad thing worse, because you may be removing powerful restraints upon evil. Your private goodness, therefore, may allow evil to flourish without restraint. That position is unfashionable among Christian thinkers today, but it is associated with some of the greatest Christians, such as Paul and Augustine. Nor does this type of dualism necessarily lead to a flight from political responsibility. It has often, in fact, led to real political commitment of a very particular sort. Those who think this way believe in the politics of amelioration. They try to make bad things better, though they may not believe it is ever possible to make them perfect. They work to achieve improvements here and there in the human situation, but they never expect to transform it into any kind of perfection of justice. Many significant improvements in human society are the result of the patience and skill of such practitioners of Christian pragmatism.

③ Very different from this group are those who identify totally with one of the world's own political philosophies, because they believe that God reveals his will through history. They seek to rally the support of Christianity for the philosophy which currently represents his will. Political philosophies take many forms, of course, so there have been many variants on this theme. One thing should be noted, however. The people in any generation who take an interest in these matters are called the intelligentsia, or the opinion-formers. They tend to be a fairly coherent group in society, and the members of the group influence and reinforce each other's attitudes. There is fashion in thought, as in everything else, and very often people adopt a position because it is fashionable and not because they have thought it through. What the best minds have thought about these matters has varied greatly, so you are presented, as you study history, with the baffling spectacle of Christian intellectuals throwing their eloquent support behind every conceivable type of political philosophy. Christian thinkers have thrown their weight behind monarchy, and provided it with theological justification, even for its more extreme pretensions, such as the divine right of kings. There has always been a strain of romantic monarchism in one strand of Catholic social thought. Another strand runs towards a kind of Christian Fascism, or the support of the strong, charismatic political figure, such as Franco, raised by God to rule. Another strong and abiding element in Christian social thought tends towards libertarianism, perhaps best represented in G. K. Chesterton's genial philosophy of Distributionism. It is too easy to dismiss these ideas today because they are dated.

What about current themes? The most popular among Christian intellectuals in the West is the enthusiastic endorsement of state socialism, as providing the best solution to the world's ills. If it was once possible to dismiss the Church as the Conservative Party at prayer, it is probably nearer the truth today to describe it as the Socialist Party at Mass. Nevertheless, there is already a strong intellectual tide running against the identification of socialism with Christianity, especially in America, where there is a spirited revival of neo-conservatism among intellectuals.

What all these groups have brought to their various supporters is a sense of vision and possibility, though their confident plans for the good society have often been wrecked by the stubborn intractability of human history. Intellectual visionaries, however, are rarely diverted by uncongenial facts. They are often imbued with a mystical sense of their own righteousness in the face of surrounding wickedness. This accounts for their tendency to pour exalted moral scorn upon those whose answers differ from their own.

In the face of 'this discord in the pact of things', how are Christians to respond to the command to minister to the needs of the world? I would like to suggest four axioms for Christians as they grapple with these problems.

First of all, I think Christians ought to recognize that there is no universally obvious political programme which can be deduced from the New Testament. There are, of course, a number of important principles or moral presumptions which can be found there, but they can be and always have been applied by Christians, thoughtfully and with a clear conscience, in a number of different ways.

Secondly, we ought to recognize that the issues which confront us in the world are amazingly complex, and a large margin of error should be allowed for in our apprehension of the situation. We are called to what Peter Berger has called 'an ethics of ignorance', in which we move about in the dark. Part of this ignorance lies in the area of sheer fact, but an equally important part lies among the consequences of our acts. Karl Popper talks about 'the unintended social consequences of intentional social acts'. These unintended consequences are often damaging, and they frequently outweigh any good our intended acts might have achieved. We must act, of course, but we must learn from *all* the consequences of our acts, and, if necessary, be prepared to change our minds.

I believe, thirdly, that Christians ought to make the most informed deductions they can from the welter of circumstances available to them, and act according to the light they have received. There should, however, be a certain level of procedural humility in the claims they make for their point of view. F. D. Maurice pointed out that 'men are usually right in what they affirm and wrong in what they deny'. It is important to affirm our point of view. It is not always wise or just to attack our neighbour's. The modern scientific discipline of conflict analysis among groups shows that it is possible for groups to survive in spite of, and to be enriched because of, opposing points of view. We must learn that the conflict of ideas is itself a part of the reality of our life together, and that it is rare indeed for one point of view to represent the whole truth.

Finally, I think that Christian leaders should be careful when they publicly espouse particular political programmes. In the midst of the baffling discords of political theory, it is unfair of them to suggest that they are proclaiming the mind of the Church as taught by Christ. There is rarely, in these matters, a clear directive from Christ to which we can appeal that might arbitrate the quarrel that has gone on among Christian thinkers for two thousand years. We confront a mystery here. Jesus seems determined to leave certain matters to us. He has provided us with a few principles. 'Now', he seems to say, 'go out into the complexities of my world and wrestle with the difficulties. Join with me in my struggle to save the world.'

Chapter 6

SUFFERING

Perceiving then that they were about to come and take him by
force to make him king, Jesus withdrew again to the hills by
himself. When evening came, his disciples went down to the sea,
got into a boat, and started across the sea to Capernaum. It was
now dark, and Jesus had not yet come to them. The sea rose
because a strong wind was blowing. When they had rowed about
three or four miles, they saw Jesus walking on the sea and drawing
near to the boat. They were frightened, but he said to them, 'It
is I; do not be afraid.' Then they were glad to take him into the
boat, and immediately the boat was at the land to which they
were going.

John 6:15–21

I have never been to the Holy Land, but the words 'the sea of
Galilee' have always been very evocative to me, as I imagine they
are to most Christians. The phrase is almost synonomous with
peace. It presents an image of warm summer afternoons, filled with
the murmur of insects, the drowsy calling of birds and the sound of
lake water lapping on the shore. Something of this mood comes
through in the line of the famous hymn, 'O Sabbath rest by Galilee'.

Apparently the picture is true, for some of the time. It is a place
of great beauty and pleasant climate; but the picture can change
dramatically in almost no time at all. The reason is obvious. The
sea of Galilee is six hundred feet below sea level. It is surrounded
by mountains, which are fissured and gorged by deep valleys
through which rivers empty themselves into the sea. These valleys
are perfect funnels for the sudden winds which come from the west.
They hurtle through the valleys on to the sea and create violent
storms. The powerful and disordered tumult of crosswinds churns

55

up the sea in all directions. The Jews were never fond of the sea at the best of times. It was unpredictable and frightening. It became for them a perfect symbol of the precariousness of life. St John the Divine, in his vision of the new heaven and the new earth in chapter twenty-one of the Book of Revelation, announced with relief that 'the sea was no more'. For obvious reasons, therefore, the stories in the Gospels about our Lord's walking on the water and stilling the storm have become parables of life itself, with its unpredictable alternation of peace and tumult, joy and tragedy. Generations of Christians have seen these stories as symbols of man's life, for our life is always threatened and frequently overwhelmed by the sudden inrush of unheralded tragedy. John encapsulates this theme from the Christian tradition in one brief and sparingly detailed miracle.

John and Mark agree in their description of the sequence of events. We are told that after the feeding of the multitude, Jesus perceived their intention to 'take him by force and make him king'. Jesus gave us his own commentary on their design. They came after him because they ate their fill of the loaves, not because they 'saw the signs'. They saw in Jesus the answer to their perception of their own needs. They projected onto him their own programme for the solution of the problems they faced. And we can be quite certain that Jesus was severely tempted to comply with their demands. We know that he was filled with compassion for the multitude in their poverty and distress. In the great temptation narratives in Matthew and Luke the demand is made with great force to turn stones into bread. It is the temptation to convert the mission of Jesus into an instrument for the cleansing and reordering of humanity's political structures. As a desirable end, it is so close to the real desire of Jesus as to present him with something of an inner crisis. The misery and injustice of the world are so offensive to God's heart that Christ was sorely tempted to submit to the world's estimate of its own needs. But is there an institutional answer to the world's needs? The answer, after many modifications of meaning, seems to me to be 'No'. It is true that institutions confirm, magnify and profoundly affect the inherent sinfulness of human nature, so Christians must be committed to the permanent reformation of all human structures. Nevertheless, history offers little support to the theory that institutional rearrangements, of themselves, can guarantee justice. All institutions become modes or carriers of human wickedness,

56

no matter how enlightened or refined. The primary source of corruption is the heart of man, and you don't efface that corruption by rearranging power blocks. That does not alter the fact of evil; it merely changes its configurations. The New Testament recognizes this. One could say that it has a minimalist view of government. It allows the magistrate the use of the sword, not for any good he can achieve, but for the restraint of evil. It can be argued, therefore, that the Christian doctrine of man's inherent sinfulness is the theory that lies behind the democratic state. Democracy does not expunge human sinfulness, but it does erect a system of checks and balances against it. While Christians have always sought to be as loyal to their nations as their consciences would allow, they have never allowed the state to claim absolute authority over them, nor have they seen in the state the answer to human sinfulness. I would be prepared to push the argument a little further and say that, where society is sufficiently developed to allow it, the democratic system of the reversibility of government is the system that is most consistent with the Christian doctrine of man. Nevertheless, Christ seems to have offered no opinion on the subject of mankind's collective arrangements and there is plenty of evidence that he refused to allow others to recruit him for their side in the everlasting debate. He seems at the same time to be both too radical and too transcendent in his approach to be diverted into a debate about structures. His approach to men and women was individual. He resisted the temptation to take the lead over multitudes. This was undoubtedly because he knew that a corrupt tree brought forth corrupt fruit, and there is little point in reorganizing the orchard if the trees are diseased. On the other hand, he also knew the profound effect that a few good men could have on society as a whole, so, implicit in his address to individuals is the whole history of the Christian struggle to make society conform as closely as possible to the Kingdom of God. Another principle can be discovered in Christ's personal approach to individuals. No matter what type of society they are born into, each generation of men and women has to recapitulate in its own private history the story of Christ's encounter with human nature. Just as the fall of man is recapitulated in each individual so is the offer of God's love made to each individual. No set of social arrangements can obviate this particularization of the drama of redemption.

But this intense personalism of Christ was balanced by his transcendentalism. He grieved over the earthly pains of his children, he was stung into anger at the cruelty and carelessness of the powerful, but he never ceased to remind his hearers that the real purpose of their living was to prepare them for eternity. 'Do not fear those who kill the body but cannot kill the soul; rather fear him who can destroy both soul and body in hell' (Matthew 10:28). 'Blessed are you when men revile you and persecute you and utter all kinds of evil against you falsely on my account. Rejoice and be glad, for your reward is great in heaven' (Matthew 5:11). For Jesus, as for Paul, our real citizenship is in heaven, and we can enjoy the privileges and joys of that citizenship even in the midst of earthly bondage.

It was this experience of enormous inner freedom that attracted the slaves and the poor into the Christian Church. Christianity is still a slaves' religion. It still preaches liberty to captives, but it is a paradoxical kind of liberty: it is liberty within the prison, not necessarily liberation from the prison. This is a frightening doctrine for a comfortable, white Western to handle, because it can be so easily used to justify his own privileges. Nevertheless, the guilt and anguish that many of us feel must not be used as an alibi for distorting the radical transcendentalism of Christ. My wealth is a problem between me and Christ. He will not let me use my guilt to engage in theological sleight of hand, whereby I substitute some human programme for the gospel. Much of that goes on in Christian circles today. For the highest of human motives, many Christians have decided to manufacture bread from stones, unlike Christ who, when they sought to make him a king, escaped into the hills to pray. As I have said, the attempt to make him a king must have faced him with an enormous moral and spiritual crisis. There must have been a real struggle against a strong desire to accede to the world's request. Faithful to his Father's mission, he turned away from the temptation, and thereby plunged generations of his followers into an enduring perplexity.

John tells us that, when the evening fell and Jesus had still not returned, the disciples got into a boat to row across the lake to Capernaum. When they were some miles out a strong wind arose. Mark tells us that 'they were distressed in rowing'. John is very sparing in the details he gives. He simply tells us that, as they rowed against the wind, they saw Jesus walking on the sea, and 'they were frightened'. No attempt is made to enhance the miracle. Indeed, several commentators wonder if John really intended to describe a miracle at all, since the phrase 'walking on the sea' can mean walking along the sea shore. They suggest that the disciples had almost reached the shore, when Jesus loomed out of the darkness on the beach. Again, very little purpose is served by the discussion. In Mark's account of what is presumably the same incident there is no doubt at all that Jesus is walking on the water. We can also be quite certain that John's reticence is not caused by any embarrassment with the miraculous nature of the event. Rather, he takes the miracle for granted in order to concentrate upon its significance. In William Temple's words, 'for St John the meaning is to be found in the peace of attainment which immediately supervenes when, tossed with trouble, we willingly receive Jesus to be our companion' (*Readings in St John's Gospel*, page 77). Devoted as I am to William Temple, I find his summation of the significance of this miracle mysteriously unsatisfying. It is partly, I think, because I know of many who have genuinely taken Jesus to be their companion, but who have rarely found the peace of attainment of which Temple speaks.

A consideration of this, the fifth miracle in John's Gospel, brings us up against one of the central mysteries of the Christian faith, the experience of suffering. By repudiating the offer of political leadership and worldly power, Christ embraced suffering as the divinely chosen instrument of salvation. There is something of a paradox here, of course, because the miracle recorded by John, of Jesus walking on the water towards the terrified disciples, is clearly meant to be a parable which teaches the presence of Jesus beside the Christian who is overwhelmed by life's tragedies. Most commentators see in it a clearly intended parallel to Psalm 107:

They that go down to the sea in ships, and occupy their business in great waters; These men see the works of the Lord, and his wonders in the deep. For at his word the stormy wind ariseth, which lifteth up the waves thereof. They are carried up to the heaven, and down again to the deep; their soul melteth away because of the trouble. They reel to and fro, and stagger like a drunken man, and are at their wits' end. So when they cry unto the Lord in their trouble, he delivereth them out of their distress. For he maketh the storm to cease, so that the waves thereof are still. Then are they glad, because they are at rest; and so he bringeth them unto the haven where they would be (verses 23–30).

There are Christians who will attest to the reality of Christ's presence beside them in the midst of life's storm. There are, too, Christians who will claim that Christ has rescued them from the storm, that he has made the storm to cease and the waves to be still. But this is not the universal testimony of Christians, and may be misleading. It is possible to present Christianity as a supernatural mission to rescue people from worldly tragedies and predicaments. This kind of triumphalist view of Christianity is very close to the expectations of his followers which Jesus repudiated. Again and again he rammed home the terrible, and to them inconceivable, truth that his victory would lie in what the world counted failure. He took every estimate of worldly success and reversed it utterly, even unto death. 'The son of man must *suffer*', he said. And this suffering was not a tactic; it was not a device to gain some sort of worldly leverage; it was not a means to some other end on earth. It was, somehow, the very mode and expression of God's relationship with the world, revealed to those who could see it. As things were between God and his children, suffering was the only appropriate expression of his love. For John, indeed, the suffering of Christ was the final and most complete revelation of his glory. The glory that had flashed forth in brief and intermittent beams in the miracles, shone with sustained radiance from the cross. 'Father, the hour has come; glorify thy Son that the Son may glorify thee' (John 17:1).

It follows from this that, for the Christian, suffering has enormous redemptive significance. Christians who face suffering must not expect any automatic remission of pain. Rather, we must seek to understand by what means the suffering itself may be transfigured into redemptive energy. We will find that Christ is present in the suffering, but that he does not always rescue us from it. Something more miraculous can happen. The suffering itself can be transcended, and become the vehicle of some new grace. These words are perilously easy to write, especially for one who has known little real suffering in his life, but they come close to the central mystery of God's way with us. But what do I mean by suffering?

My meaning is this: suffering is the endurance and acceptance of anything which we have no power to change. It is the unavoidability of suffering that I want to look at. Life is a web of necessities which we must endure, must suffer, if we would catch even a glimpse of the meaning of things. There are many things we must change, just as there are many things we cannot change; and it is a mature wisdom that can tell the difference. I want to look at what cannot be changed, and I want to begin by looking at human communities.

In any humane and mature community, men and women have to adjust to the frustrations imposed upon them by the freedom of others to differ from them. In any normally varied community there are many differing views about many of the aspects of the common life, and no single viewpoint can ever be entirely satisfied. All must be held in an equilibrium of mutual dissatisfaction. A mature society recognizes that in a mixed community there has to be an operating compromise at work, if men and women are not constantly to be at each other's throats. We must, in fact, suffer. We must endure the fact that many people differ from us in all sorts of ways. It is a mark of a mature society when differences are allowed and an overall balance is achieved. It is a mark of intolerance, which is the refusal to suffer disagreement, when one group insists on getting its own way. This has always been the mark of the totalitarian. Tolerance, the ability to allow, to suffer a number of views to coexist, is bourgeois. In the promised land of far left or far right fantasy, only one view will prevail. This is what Professor Marcuse calls 'selective tolerance', which is merely a codeword for intolerance, the doctrine that only the elect have rights. One of the marks of our time is an increase in this kind of intolerance, an impatience with suffering, a refusal to accept unalterable differences. If we are to retain humane political structures in the West we must learn to suffer, to endure, to live within the tensions of passionately held disagreements. We must suffer thus, if society is to endure.

And we must also learn to suffer the limitations of our own personality and selfhood. There is an unavoidable givenness about life, rough hew it how we will. We cannot by striving add one cubit to our stature. Maturity often begins at the point where we accept our own limitations and weaknesses. We cannot always change

61

them. We must suffer them, and often in the suffering, the acceptance of them, a new serenity is found. I do not want to caricature modern medicine or psychiatry, but there is a tendency at work today for people to give up the responsibility for their own health into the hands of experts. Ivan Illich calls this 'the expropriation of health', the taking over of what properly is my responsibility by experts. People are less prepared to suffer, to endure life. They want life purged of all discomfort, all regret. But as human beings we are heirs to all sorts of pains and limitations which are part of the very meaning of our nature. We must needs suffer them and live our lives through them, if we are to be fully human, fully alive.

Finally, we must suffer the inescapable certainty of death. 'Men must endure their going hence.' And it is death which is our greatest enemy, the symbol of everything for which we mourn, and how are we to suffer it? It is the endless endingness of things which afflicts us; all that coming to an end, all that going down into the grave, that inexorable tramp towards oblivion. How are we to suffer it? How are we to suffer the dominion of death?

Well, there is no form of words that will help us, no explanation that will do for us. Instead, there are times and places where the meaning breaks through and endurance is fortified. For Victor Gollancz it happened in some passages of some of Beethoven's last quartets. Others have found the power to endure in other ways. For Christians, it comes through many different flashes of revelation, many signs of a glory that lies concealed. For many, it has come, above all, in the image of Christ coming across troubled waters and strengthening them for the passage. 'It is I; be not afraid.'

Chapter 7

REVELATION

As he passed by, he saw a man blind from his birth. And his disciples asked him, 'Rabbi, who sinned, this man or his parents, that he was born blind?' Jesus answered, 'It was not that this man sinned, or his parents, but that the works of God might be made manifest in him. We must work the works of him who sent me, while it is day; night comes, when no one can work. As long as I am in the world, I am the light of the world.' As he said this, he spat on the ground and made clay of the spittle and anointed the man's eyes with the clay, saying to him, 'Go, wash in the pool of Siloam' (which means Sent). So he went and washed and came back seeing.

John 9:1–7

Since the gospel writers cannot yet answer us back, it is temptingly easy to put thoughts into their minds or words into their mouths. It is, for instance, very tempting to read into John's account of the seven great signs a systematic account of the Christian life. Did John intend us to do this? I think it is likely, but his intentions are not really all that should concern us, anyway. Inspired writings of any sort are richer and more profound than their authors' intentions; 'they speak wiser than they know', in T. S. Eliot's words. All ages are equidistant from eternity, so any writing that has somehow captured the truth of God will be contemporary for every generation. While we must never lose sight of the fact that the New Testament is a primary witness to certain historic facts, we can be equally confident that its primary use for us is the elucidation of our own condition. Through it, Christ, our divine contemporary, makes his approach to us. In the seven great signs of glory in John's

63

Gospel, Christ illuminates the human condition and its needs and longings.

At the wedding at Cana in Galilee Christ affirmed our search for joy in the natural creation. At the same time, however, he taught us that the creation raises a desire in us for what it does not itself fully supply.

The healing of the nobleman's son takes us a stage further. What we long for lies beyond ourselves, though there is, in each of us, a disposition towards it, a sort of preparatory impulse. Nevertheless, to receive what we long for requires an act of surrender and obedience.

At Bethzatha, the healing of the crippled man reminded us that there is something else present in our nature. Alongside the pull of joy which draws us from ourselves and prompts us to submit to the word of Christ, there is another force at work, pulling us back into ourselves. The gift of joy requires from us a painful response of willed obedience to the one who stands before us.

When we make the act of faith and give our assent, we are not left alone. By his feeding of the multitude Christ reminds us that we are nourished by the supernatural reality of his presence. Christ made the same point in another way, when he commanded us to abide in him as a branch abides in the vine.

Nevertheless, this mystical intimacy with Christ does not shelter us from the shocks and sorrows of history. However, by his walking on the water towards his frightened disciples, Christ reminds us that he is present with us throughout the storms of time.

In the sixth sign we return, with a subtle difference of emphasis, to the theme of faith which was set forth in the second sign, the healing of the nobleman's son. Both of these signs point to the most fundamental theological category in Christian thought, revelation. We could easily argue that revelation is the theme of John's Gospel. It is dangerous to categorize, but there has always been a useful distinction made in Christian thought between 'natural' and 're-vealed' theology. The former has been that area of religion which man can discover unaided except by his reason. This begs the question, of course. Can there be any knowledge of the things of God which is not, in some way, prompted by God himself, if only by the creation of the very disposition that asks religious questions? The distinction between natural and revealed theology, therefore, cannot be held to be absolute; nevertheless, it is of value. By revelation is meant those special or miraculous overtures from God which are the centre of the Christian claim. We have seen, however, that even this special or particular approach of God is ambiguous. Indeed, the main burden of John's Gospel is a sad recognition of this fateful ambiguity: 'He was in the world and the world was made by him, and the world knew him not.' The approach of God is not always met by a corresponding welcome in humanity. Effective revelation requires two conditions. The primary condition is obviously the divine action itself, the overture or intervention of God. But this overture does not produce an automatic response. It is only effective if it is correctly interpreted or understood by those to whom it comes. In the healing of the nobleman's son there was a strong emphasis upon the human response. The man believed the word of Jesus and went back to Capernaum at his command. In the healing of the man born blind there is a different emphasis. Here the divine act is the central element in the encounter. The discontinuity is stressed. The tragic and lifelong blindness of the man is emphasized. John wants us to recognize the miraculous surprise and newness of Christian faith. In Hoskyns' words, 'To become a Christian is not to recover what has been lost, but to receive a wholly new illumination' (*The Fourth Gospel*, p. 352). It is this new illumination which is the central focus of the sixth sign.

The encounter begins with a characteristic repudiation by Jesus of abstract theology. We find little thought or speculation for its own sake in Jesus, no abstract theorizing. Indeed, much of his anger was expressed against those in whom speculation and cerebration had become dominant characteristics, usually at the expense of the poor and the simple. 'Rabbi, who sinned, this man or his parents, that he was born blind?' It was widely held in our Lord's day that suffering was due to sin. The general principle was laid down by R. Ammi: 'There is no death without sin, and there is no suffering without iniquity' (Quoted in *The Gospel According to John*, Leon Morris, p. 478). Jesus always displayed impatience with this kind of metaphysical parlour game. He cut through rabbinical disputations with blunt and authoritative directness. He was concerned with action, with making a difference to the human situation not in debating its causes.

'It was not that this man had sinned, or his parents, but that the works of God might be made manifest in him. We must work the works of him who sent me, while it is day; night comes, when no one can work.' Of course, Jesus does not rule out the possibility that suffering can be the result of sin. His warning to the cripple who lay at the pool of Bethzatha implies that there was, in his case, a connection between his suffering and his conduct: 'See, you are well! Sin no more, that nothing worse befall you' (5:14). But even in this encounter his purpose is entirely practical. He is intent upon restoring the man's lost powers. Our Lord's work was essentially pastoral and redemptive, not philosophical. This is still the primary work of the Church. When Christian theology is separated from the pastoral and redemptive task of the Church it runs the risk of ceasing to be gospel and becoming, instead, just another branch of disputable human learning. The purpose of Jesus was to change the world, not explain it.

Even as he engaged in this little encounter with his disciples, Jesus was preparing to heal the man born blind. Using a traditional healing method, he made a clay from his own spittle and the dust of the earth, and smeared the man's eyes with the clay. The restoring of sight to the blind is one of the most consistent parts of the tradition about Jesus. The actual miracle reported here is startling enough and gives us plenty to think about; nevertheless it is probably true that John intended us to find significance in the details of the story as well as in its conclusion. Many commentators find the action of anointing the blind man with clay an allusion to the creation of man from the dust of the earth in the book of Genesis. Hoskyns quotes Quesnel as saying: 'He who made man out of the earth cures him with earth.' The Fathers also saw enormous significance in the name of the pool to which the blind man was sent by Jesus. The pool was called Siloam or 'Sent' because the water was originally 'sent' into the pool by means of a conduit. Jesus is frequently described as 'He whom the Father has sent'. Hoskyns agrees with the Fathers that John intended an identification of Siloam with Christ. He goes on: '. . . the waters of Siloam disappear in the living water of Christ . . . in Christian baptism and in that purification and illumination which formed both the starting point and the permanent background of primitive Christian experience' (*The Fourth Gospel*, p. 355).

However the details of the miracle are explained, there can be little doubt that John intended us to see in it the revelation of Jesus as the glory of God and the light of the world. Jesus is set forth as the revelation of God in whom men are to believe. This raises one of the most basic and vexing questions for the Christian believer. How is faith achieved? Why is one person brought to faith and not another? The answer seems to be that there is in mankind a predisposition towards faith, a sort of latent belief. John calls it 'the true light that enlightens every man'. Whatever you call this sense that lies within us, it sends us searching and questioning for the meaning and purpose of things. We cannot find that meaning in the creation itself, because it is part of the very riddle we are trying to read. However, something of that meaning comes through the creation in hints and rumours. Some news of that thing we seek comes filtering through to us, though we know not how. But these very hints and signs only increase our frustration. We cannot tell how much genuinely comes from the source of meaning and how much comes from ourselves. It seems that this sense, this longing within us, raises a desire for what it does not itself fully supply. And so it places us, in Newman's phrase, 'on the look-out for revelation'. We know that we need an authoritative disclosure of God in order to still our questions and satisfy our longings.

However, it has to be admitted that not everyone is on the look-out. The predisposition towards faith is stronger in some than in others. Indeed, there seem to be some people in whom it does not exist at all. Nevertheless, this latent faith, this disposition towards faith, is probably not as rare as the clergy are frequently tempted to believe. David Martin once perciperently remarked: ' "Modern man" is a clergyman's friend who has just lost his faith.' Several recent opinion polls in Britain and America have revealed a surprisingly high incidence of what might be called mystical experience among members of the public. Nevertheless, it does seem to be the case that in most people this predisposition towards faith is very frail and indecisive. In a 'believing' culture such people will go along with the dominant belief without real personal conviction. In an unbelieving culture they will revert to a mild and good-natured disbelief. Newman describes them in this way:

They are contented with themselves; they think themselves as happily conditioned as they can be under the circumstances; they only wish to be left alone; they have no need of priest or prophet; they live in their own way and in their own home, pursuing their own tastes, never looking out of doors; perhaps with natural virtues, perhaps not, but with no distinct or consistent religious sense. Thus they live, and thus they die. Such is the character of the many, all over the earth; they live, to all appearance, in some object of this world, and never rise above the world, and, it is plain, have nothing of those dispositions at all which lead to faith (*Sermons Preached on Various Occasions*, p. 68).

In John's language: 'He came unto his own and his own received him not'.

The ultimate destiny of such complaisant unbelievers is not a question we can answer, and it is probably one which Christ would refuse to answer. He will not allow us to divert our energies into metaphysical generalities. 'Are there many that be saved?' The answer always comes back in the personal mode. The question is always returned unopened to the sender, and stamped: 'What is that to thee? Follow thou me' (21:22). When Christ confronts the person in whom the light of longing already burns, a real meeting takes place. There is a moment of recognition, followed by an act of surrender. The revelation is made by God and received by man.

But the focus in the healing of the man born blind is not upon the human predisposition towards faith, leading us to be on the look-out for revelation: it is upon the nature and authority of the One who is revealed. It is the disclosure of God which is stressed, not the response of man. This reminds us, again, of the fundamental objectivity of Christian doctrine. As Paul kept reminding his converts, the gospel comes by revelation; it is not a human construction which we can alter as we will. This is what we mean by the authority of Christian doctrine. The word 'authority' may have an unfortunate ring to it in these egalitarian times, so a modern paraphrase may help. The word 'exploitation' is often used nowadays to describe a certain type of relation between men and women. When you exploit a woman you use her to your own advantage or gratification. She is not treated as a person with a unique and sacred identity, but simply as a means to some purpose you have, whether it be domestic convenience or sexual gratification. The opposite of exploitation is reverence. When you show reverence to a woman you allow her to reveal her nature to you in all its richness and need. She becomes, not a means to your gratification, but an end which has its own integrity and which you must respect. When a relationship of mutual reverence or respect is established, each discloses their inner nature to the other and the whole of life is enriched.

Now, this is a very apt parable of the Christian revelation. It is the action of God as he shows himself to us, but it is an action which is vulnerable to our indifference and can be a victim of our exploitation. It is very easy to ignore its integrity, its intrinsic authority, its interior authenticity, just as we can ignore these things in another human being. When that happens we exploit the gospel, we do not reverence it. We must first allow it to be in its own right before we can safely begin to relate to it. We must, in some sense, submit ourselves to its reality before it can be real for us. Unfortunately, this is the very reverse of the modern way. Theologians ask, not, 'What does this mean?', but, 'What meaning can I find in this?' We all ask, not, 'What demands does this make upon me and the way I live?' but, 'What adjustments must I make to this in order to fit it into the way I live?' In this way we remove both the intellectual and the ethical difficulties of the revelation, but we have done a very peculiar thing which, in the end, leaves us poorer than we were before. After all, Christianity is a voluntary relationship. We are free to refuse it, free to deny that it is true, just as we can deny the overtures of a particular person who wishes to enter our life. What is perverse and finally self-defeating, is to appear to accept it while we are, in fact, simply exploiting it to our own advantage. This destroys our integrity as well as the integrity of the revelation.

Christianity, for those who receive it, offers a wholly new illumination of the meaning of existence. It throws new light upon the nature of God and his plan for the universe. The source of that light and the agent of that plan is Jesus Christ. In Paul's words, God plans to 'sum up all things in Christ', to draw all mankind into the divine nature through him. And this divine gift is offered to each soul that opens itself to receive it. The light that lightens every man with the frail and fitful illumination of conscience and longing, breaks, at last, upon us in the full glory of revelation. In the great words of John Donne:

He brought light out of darkness, not out of a lesser light; he can bring thy Summer out of Winter, though thou have no Spring; though in the wayes of fortune, or understanding, or conscience, thou have been benighted till now, wintred and frozen, clouded and eclypsed, damped and benummed, smothered and stupefied till now, now God comes to thee, not as in the dawning of the day, not as in the bud of the spring, but as the Sun at noon to illustrate all shadowes, as the sheaves in harvest, to fill all penuries, all occasions invite his mercies, and all times are his seasons (*Sermon Preached on Christmas Day*, 1624).

Chapter 8

RESURRECTION

Then Jesus, deeply moved again, came to the tomb; it was a cave, and a stone lay upon it. Jesus said, 'Take away the stone.' Martha, the sister of the dead man, said to him, 'Lord, by this time there will be an odour, for he has been dead four days.' Jesus said to her, 'Did I not tell you that if you would believe you would see the glory of God?' So they took away the stone. And Jesus lifted up his eyes and said, 'Father I thank thee that thou hast heard me. I knew that thou hearest me always, but I have said this on account of the people standing by, that they may believe that thou didst send me.' When he had said this, he cried with a loud voice, 'Lazarus, come out.' The dead man came out, his hands and feet bound with bandages, and his face wrapped with a cloth. Jesus said to them, 'Unbind him, and let him go.'

John 11:38–44

The last day of June in 1976 was a warm and lovely day in the city of Edinburgh. I remember this day well, because it was the day my mother died. I got on the train to travel to the West of Scotland and I sat there in the hot railway carriage, reading the office of the dead and holding in my grief. My world had come to a strange stop, yet the rest of the world did not notice. That was the most perplexing thing about it. I wanted the world to stop and mark this passing, but it did not. Hundreds were sunbathing in Princes Street Gardens as I boarded the train; and as I looked out of the window everything was happening as usual. No one knew or took any notice; they worked on, joyful in the heat, or they sailed boats on Linlithgow Loch as the train passed through. The world had ended for me, not for them. It seemed extraordinary to me. Yet I was not surprised,

71

for I had noticed all this before. Priests are present at many a dying, and they lay the dead in their final resting place. I have noticed hundreds of times that as the dead are brought into church or driven through the streets, the world goes on as usual. The buses still run, people hurry to work, shoppers gaze into store windows. For them it is of no moment, yet behind me sit the mourners, enclosed in that isolating sorrow that cuts you off from the rest of the world. Death is everywhere and over all, but the world does not, cannot notice. The trains continue to run on time, men walk up the front path and pick up the daily paper, and the voices of children cry out somewhere in the street. The world has stopped for some, yet the world runs on and the dying continues. Our grief cries to the world to stop once, to bow its head, to order silence, but time and its children run on heedlessly. W. H. Auden captures this strange dislocation in 'Musée des Beaux Arts':

About suffering they were never wrong,
The Old Masters: how well they understood
Its human position; how it takes place
While someone else is eating or opening a window or just
    walking dully along;
How, when the aged are reverently, passionately waiting
For the miraculous birth, there always must be
Children who did not specially want it to happen, skating
On a pond at the edge of the wood:
They never forgot
That even the dreadful martyrdom must run its course
Anyhow in a corner, some untidy spot
Where the dogs go on with their doggy life and the torturer's
    horse
Scratches its innocent behind on a tree.

No, the world does not notice, but there is always one who does. The world may mark the death of princes and order the firing of muskets into the silent air. There is only one who marks the death of paupers, one who is there at every unregarded grave and leads all who are made little by death into his own marvellous light. We know this because of the death of Lazarus of Bethany, the brother of Martha and Mary, who were all friends of Jesus.

John wants us to understand two miracles in his account of the

72

seventh and last sign which Jesus did. There is a small miracle and a miracle so vast it defies comprehension and calls to our faith. With the small miracle we ought not to waste much time, though much ink has been wasted upon it. John himself offers little in the way of explanation beyond his description of the facts. The small miracle is the raising of Lazarus from the dead. John gives us a detailed and explicit description of what happened, and he lays considerable emphasis upon the central fact. The tradition of those days was that for three days the spirit hovered over its own corpse, unsure of its final release. In that time there might be a reviving. Lazarus, John tells us, had been dead for four days when Jesus got there. That is why Martha was reluctant to open the tomb; the stench of decomposition would have been overpowing. Lazarus was truly and definably dead, yet Jesus called him forth from the tomb and restored him, alive, to his family. We cannot tell how he did it, any more than we can tell how the Word of God created the universe and made life in the beginning. John does not argue. The giver and source of life could restore life. The Word of God who called creation into being by his command, 'Let there be', could call Lazarus forth from the non-being of death by another creative command. It is, after all, a small miracle compared to that original act at the beginning of all things. Nevertheless, we ought to pay some attention to the difficulties the critics have raised.

The main objection which has been raised against the truth of this miracle is that there is no mention of it in the other Gospels. Surely, it is argued, an event as momentous as this and one which, it is claimed, lay behind the determination of the authorities to kill Jesus, would have been mentioned by the other gospel writers if it had happened? The silence of the other evangelists is certainly a problem, but it is one of many problems with which we must live, because there is no satisfactory solution to it. We cannot tell why the other writers do not mention this event. If you resolve the problem by concluding that it did not happen, you only create a more profound problem. The silence of the synoptics is a historical problem. If you clear that problem up by deciding that John has given us a fictitious narrative, you substitute an intractable moral problem for a straightforward historical one. John claims that he is giving us history. We can be quite certain that it is history which has been meditated upon. We know, too, that history is always facts plus interpretation. John claims to be giving us much more than history, but can we honestly assert that he is giving us less? For an event to *mean* something it must first *be* something. John clearly teaches that the events of the life of Jesus were revelatory, but he is most insistent upon their historical reality. Indeed, many critics believe that the main purpose of his writing was to assert the truth of the claim that the Word had really come in the flesh and was not some sort of phantasm or abstraction. One of the current philosophies of John's day held that matter was inherently evil. For this reason one could not speak of a true incarnation of the Word of God, but only of an apparent one. The Word of God did not really come in the flesh, but only *seemed* to do so. This heresy is called Docetism, from the Greek *doceo*, 'to seem'. Against this, John proclaimed the historical actuality of the incarnation. The paradox of much modern criticism of John is that it turns his purpose on its head. By claiming that John's historical narratives are carefully fabricated vehicles for conveying theological messages, they produce a modern version of the Docetism which John set out to oppose. To reject the historical nature of the raising of Lazarus creates more problems than it solves.

But it is not impossible, anyway, to provide some reasons for the silence of the synoptics on the subject. I suspect that most of the critics who reject this miracle because it does not appear in the other evangelists, really reject it on *a priori* grounds. They reject miracles in general or raisings of the dead in particular. If this is the case, then the synoptics will offer them cold comfort. It is a firm part of the gospel tradition that Jesus raised the dead. There are three places in the synoptics where the fact is mentioned.

When John the Baptist sent from prison to enquire whether Jesus were the Christ, we are told that Jesus sent a message back to him: 'Go and tell John what you hear and see: the blind receive their sight and the lame walk, lepers are cleansed and the deaf hear, and the dead are raised up, and the poor have good news preached to them' (Matthew 11:4). All the synoptics give an account of the raising of the daughter of Jairus (Mark 5:21–43), and Luke gives an account of the raising of a widow's son in the city of Nain (Luke 7:11–17). Whatever reasons there are for the silence of the synoptic gospels about the raising of Lazarus, therefore, it cannot be because

74

of any doubt on their part about the power of Jesus to raise the dead.

It is just conceivable that Lazarus was still alive when Mark wrote his Gospel, and he did not wish to embarrass him by reporting the event. More compelling is the fact that Peter is not mentioned in John's Gospel between 6:68 and 13:6. There is a similar gap in Matthew and Luke. It has been traditionally held that the reminiscences of Peter lie behind Mark's Gospel. It is conceivable, therefore, that Peter was not present at the raising of Lazarus, having stayed behind in Galilee when the others went up to Jerusalem, where he joined them before the Passover. Support for the view that Peter was absent from this event is provided by the fact that Thomas is the spokesman for the apostles in verse sixteen, just after Jesus has announced his intention to go to Bethany where his friend lies dead. It is possible that Mark does not mention the miracle because it was not part of Peter's reminiscenses.

It seems to me, therefore, that there are no absolutely convincing reasons for rejecting this miracle on historical grounds. The only valid reasons for rejecting it are philosophical, but on those grounds the whole Christian tradition can be rejected. Even so, John wants us to do more than focus on the miraculous nature of this event. It is for him much more than an astounding miracle. It is revelation. Sir Edwyn Hoskyns makes this point with particular clarity:

> These miraculous actions are not introduced as proofs of a doctrine or as symbolical illustrations of Christian mysticism; they constitute the revelation of the power of Jesus, and the truth is manifested in His historical action. The supremacy of Christian faith is thus shown to rest upon decisive actions in the human life of Jesus. The purpose of the author is not to record crises in the life of Jesus in order to explain historically why the Jews put Him to death, but to isolate important actions of Jesus and to display them as providing a firm foundation of Christian faith (Hoskyns, op. cit., p. 395).

The raising of Lazarus from the grave to continue his earthly life for a little longer is a sign of something much more wonderful than the restoration of bodily life. It is a sign of a much greater miracle, the promise of that eternal life which death cannot touch. To that greater miracle we must now turn.

75

John tells us at the beginning of his book that no man has ever seen God, but that the only Son, who is in the very heart of God, has made him known in history. That is a very good definition of revelation. What we are unable to see for ourselves God makes known to us. The two great mysteries which confront us are God and death, and the life of Jesus Christ illuminates the darkness of both of them. Jesus showed us much about the hidden nature of God; he revealed his glory. He also lit up the darkness of the other great mystery which confronts us, by irradiating the awefulness of death with the power of his own life. We would like to know much more than we do, of course. We would like Christ, in John Donne's phrase, to illustrate all shadows, like the Sun at noon. That he does not do. He gives us enough light to walk by, never enough to illumine all mysteries. He told those who believed there was no resurrection that God was God of the living, not of the dead. By that strange statement he meant that the dead were not dead to God. He was still the God of Abraham, and the God of Isaac, and the God of Jacob (Mark 12:26). But it is in John that we are allowed to see a little farther into the mystery. It is in John that we find the promises which have followed Christians to their graves since the dawn of the Church.

When Martha met Jesus outside Bethany he comforted her with words that are used at every Christian burial: 'I am the resurrection and the life'. The most moving commentary on that text is provided by the apostle Paul in his Letter to the Philippians. Paul wrote this letter on Death Row while he was in prison in Rome. He was awaiting trial, facing possible execution, and he was musing upon his situation. Most men in that situation would enlarge upon their hopes for freedom, the success of their latest appeal, the activity of their lawyers on their behalf. The paradox in Paul's case is that he would rather the situation issued in his death. Then he would be with his beloved Lord. 'It is my eager expectation and hope that I shall not be at all ashamed, but that with full courage now as always Christ will be honoured in my body, whether by life or by death. For to me to live is Christ, and to die is gain . . . My desire is to depart and be with Christ' (Philippians 1:20–3). Christ was a dominating reality for Paul. For him he really was 'the life'. For most of us Christ is more a matter of longing than of real presence. He is a tantalizing possibility, not a blazing reality. He is always

76

just ahead of us, turning the corner before we can catch up. For Paul it was different. Christ was his whole life, and since Christ was no longer time- and earth-bound, but an eternal reality who brought the beyond into the very midst of the earth, it followed that the full enjoyment of Christ was yet to come. It lay after death, in heaven. So Paul was eager to die, in order to be with Christ fully, the way a man longs to marry in order to be with his beloved always.

This rumination of Paul's is baffling to most of us. It is completely at odds with the whole tenor of our society, where death is thought of as the ultimate disaster which is to be postponed as long as possible. I have to confess that I am strongly affected by the world's attitude. I can't say what Paul said, nor can I entirely believe what Jesus said, though I long to. One reason I am a Christian, therefore, is because I want to learn how to die. We could say that one of the purposes of the Church is to teach us how to die. It teaches us not to hold on to things, not even people. It wants us to learn how to die to all things earthly, in order to prepare us for the grand renunciation of our own final journey. The Church knows our terror of dying, so it teaches us by all sorts of little deaths, to get us used to giving things up. But it does something more positive than that. It asks us to see the world aright. To look through it to what abides. It reminds us that we are all looking for a beauty and permanence we never find completely in this life. That, whispers the Church, is our longing for God and the beauty of him. The saints have known that longing and known that its solace is not found here, which is why, like Paul, they long to depart and be with Christ. When good Bishop Gore lay dying he looked up with blazing eyes and whispered 'transcendent glory', and fell asleep in Christ, his eyes already dazzled by the beauty he was soon to possess. Like Paul he had grown close to Christ in a long life, so that for him to live was Christ and to die was to gain abundant life, for Christ was resurrection and life.

By his promise to Martha and by the raising of her brother, Jesus showed us, in our fear, that he was the life who is lord of death. When we fall asleep in death, therefore, there will be no waking in a strange place. Instead, there will be the Christ for whom we have all along been searching. John confirms this promise of eternal life by what he reports of our Lord's words during his farewell discourse. In chapter fourteen he gives us the other great promise which has comforted Christians as they have gazed into the inconsolable loss of death:

> Let not your hearts be troubled; believe in God, believe also in me. In my Father's house are many rooms; if it were not so, would I have told you that I go to prepare a place for you? And when I go and prepare a place for you, I will come again and will take you to myself, that where I am you may be also (14:1–3).

It has been suggested by William Temple that behind this assurance lies the tradition of the Eastern caravan. Whenever an important journey was taken in the East, a guide or scout was sent on ahead to prepare the evening's camp. The travellers would arrive at their resting place and find all prepared for them, so that they could immediately find peace and comfort. So the assurance means that Christ has been ahead of us to all our resting places, and prepared them for us. We find the same image used in the twelfth chapter of the Letter to the Hebrews, where it is claimed that Christ is 'the pioneer and finisher of our faith'. Christ has gone on ahead of us to prepare the way for us. He has been through everything that faces us, and prepared it for us.

This teaching certainly applies to our life here on earth, but perhaps the most momentous implication of it is the promise of eternity, of heaven, the promise that our journey will end in the embrace of our Father and the full freedom of deep heaven. And what can we say of heaven? This only. Why are we afraid to die? In my own case it is because of the loss of so much I hold dear: all the beauty of the earth, the love of family and friend, the light flickering in a dark church on a quiet Easter dawn. So I cling to these things, fearful of losing them. But what are all these things, if not the moving image of eternity, pale promises of heaven itself, foreshadowing of a belonging and a homeland where there is no loss or shadow of change? In heaven I shall have the real and enduring joy of these things to a degree unimaginable. No wonder Paul wanted to depart, was impatient to die, to find the unchanging reality behind this heartbreakingly beautiful yet incomplete life.

And this is what awaits us. So there is no loss in death, only gain and glory and joy unspeakable. This knowledge does not make us pale and pining and useless to the world: it liberates us to live in this world with a careless joy and detachment. If only today's Church could capture that spirit, could hear the strong promise of the Christ who is resurrection and life and who has gone on to prepare a place for us! If only we could rediscover the joy of what lies in store!

> There we shall be still and see; we shall see and we shall love and we shall praise. Behold what will be, in the end without end! For what is our end but to reach that kingdom which has no end? (St Augustine, *City of God*, xxii.30)

BIBLIOGRAPHY

Auden, W. H., 'Musée des Beaux Arts' from *Collected Poems*. New York, Random House, 1968; London, Faber and Faber, 1968.

Augustine, St, *The City of God*. New York and London, Oxford University Press, 1963.

Chesterton, G. K., *Stories, Essays and Poems*. London, J. M. Dent, 1946.

De Chardin, T., *The Divine Milieu*. New York, Harper and Bros, 1960; British title: *Le Divin Milieu*, London, Collins Fontana, 1969.

De Montalembert, C. F. R., *The Monks of the West*, vol. i. New York and London, Longmans, Green, 1896.

Donne, J., *Complete Poetry and Selected Prose*. New York, Modern Library, 1952; London, Nonesuch Press, 1941.

Eliot, T. S., *The Complete Poems and Plays*. New York, Harcourt, Brace, 1952; London, Faber and Faber, 1969.

Epstein, I., ed., *The Babylonian Talmud*, vol. i. London, Soncino Press, 1935.

Gore, C., *The Epistle to the Ephesians*. London, John Murray, 1909.

Greene, G., *The Power and the Glory*. New York, Viking Press, 1958; London, Heinemann, 1971.

Horwood, F. C., ed. *A. E. Housman: Poetry and Prose: A Selection*. London, Hutchinson Educational, 1972.

Hoskyns, E. C. and Davey, F. N., *The Fourth Gospel*. USA, Allenson, 1956; London, Faber and Faber, 1956.

Illich, I., *Medical Nemesis*. New York, Bantam, 1977; British title: *Limits to Medicine. Medical Nemesis: The Expropriation of Health*. London, Boyars, 1976.

Lewis, C. S., *Miracles*. London, Collins Fontana, 1967.

Lewis, C. S., *The Weight of Glory*. Grand Rapids, Eerdmans, 1965; London, SPCK, 1954.

Morris, L., *The Gospel According to John: New International Commentary*, ed. F. F. Bruce. Grand Rapids, Eerdmans, 1970; London, Marshall, Morgan and Scott, 1974.

Newman, J. H., *Apologia pro Vita Sua*. Westminster, USA, Christian Classics, 1973; London, Longmans, Green, 1895.

—, *Sermons Preached on Several Occasions*. Westminster, USA, Christian Classics, 1968; London, Longmans, Green, 1895.

Newsome, D., *On the Edge of Paradise*. University of Chicago Press, 1980. (The diary of A. C. Benson is in the Old Library of Magdalene College, Cambridge.)

Niebuhr, H. R., *Christ and Culture*. New York, Harper and Bros, 1956.

Prestige, G. L., *Life of Charles Gore*. London, Heinemann, 1935.

Smith, H. Maynard, *Frank, Bishop of Zanzibar*. London, SPCK, 1926.

Temple, W., *Readings in St John's Gospel*. London, Macmillan, 1959.

Thompson, F., 'Epilogue to "A Judgement in Heaven"' in *Works of Francis Thompson, Poems*, vol i. London, Burns, Oates and Washbourne, 1913.

Trevor, M., *Light in Winter*. London, Macmillan, 1962, quoting a speech by Cardinal Newman in Rome, 12 May 1879.

Waddell, H., *Mediaeval Latin Lyrics*. London, Constable, 1966.

Ward, W., *The Life of John Henry, Cardinal Newman*, vol. i. New York and London, Longmans, Green, 1912.

Waugh, E., *Brideshead Revisited*. New York, Dell [n.d]. London, Penguin, 1970.

Whittier, J. G. 'Dear Lord and Father of Mankind', in *English Hymnal*, Oxford University Press, 1933.